THE
INSTANT
CURRICULUM

THE INSTANT CURRICULUM

500 Developmentally Appropriate
Learning Activities for
Busy Teachers of Young Children

Pam Schiller
and Joan Rossano

Illustrations By Kathleen Kerr

Gryphon House
Mt. Rainier, Maryland

©1990 by Pam Schiller and Joan Rossano

Published by Gryphon House, Inc., 3706 Otis Street,
Mt. Rainier, Maryland 20712.
ISBN 0-87659-124-1
Library of Congress Catalog Number: 90-81885

Design: Graves Fowler Associates

To

Richele & Tiffany Schiller

Adam & Matthew Rossano

and Lee Wright

May your lives be filled with the wonder of wonder

— P.S. and J.R.

Contents

The Month-by-Month Guide to The Instant Curriculum Starts on Page 373

CHAPTER ONE

Bringing the Inside Out — Self-Expression Through Art

CHAPTER FOUR

Expanding Understanding— Developing Language Arts Skills

Month-by-Month Activity Guide Is On

Page 373

CHAPTER FIVE

First Things First — Making Math Meaningful

Month-by-Month Activity Guide Is On

Page 373

CHAPTER SIX

Music — Anywhere and Everywhere

CHAPTER SEVEN

The Wonder of Wonder — Critical Thinking and Problem Solving Skills

· ·

CHAPTER EIGHT

Moving Beyond the Horizon — Developing an Interest in Science

· ·

Month-by-Month Activity Guide Is On

Page 373

· ·

CHAPTER NINE

Everyone's a Piece of the Puzzle — An Approach to Social Studies

Introduction

This book is intended to serve as a curriculum guide and resource for teachers who plan and conduct comprehensive early childhood programs. The activities are designed to use materials readily available in most classrooms. Implementation of this curriculum does not require the teacher to spend excessive time in preparation, nor money for purchase. Underlying the planning of this book is the basic belief that children should be actively involved in the learning process and that learning experiences are not isolated. Children learn from everything they do.

The chapters represent the primary areas of a good early childhood curriculum. Each chapter begins with an overview providing the basic philosophy behind that particular curriculum area. The activities are designed to encourage the development of skills and concepts.

The focus on concepts and skills provides a flexible format that allows teachers to broaden concepts to other areas of the curriculum (integrated learning) and to utilize teachable moments for further skill and concept development. For example, the play store used in the Social Studies curriculum also has learning potential for Math (counting pennies) and Dramatic Play (role playing). A Language Arts teachable moment might occur when a child asks for help in making a grocery list. Amplification of the Teachable Moment concept is presented at the end of this introduction.

Although an activity is assigned to a specific area, its potential is not limited to that area. In the early childhood classroom, learning is integrated. For example, to develop the concept of four (Math curriculum area), a teacher using an integrated approach will provide opportunities to clap-count four (Music), to collect four leaves on a nature walk (Science) or to use four colors on a collage (Art).

A special feature of this book is the inclusion of a chapter on problem solving and critical thinking. Although problem solving and critical thinking activities have been included within each curriculum area, this chapter focuses on the potential application of these skills to all areas of learning due to the significance it holds for a child's success in a changing world.

Throughout the book, emphasis has been placed on allowing children to learn at their own level of development and progress accordingly. Emphasis has also been placed on providing choices for children to make and on letting children experiment and discover. In this way, young children will develop skills in learning how to learn and will feel confident in their ability. Learning will become an interesting process, one that continues for a lifetime.

Using Teachable Moments

The alert and interested teacher can take advantage of opportunities that arise during the day to help the children develop skills and concepts that will increase their understanding of their world. The following are a few examples:

Child	*Teacher*
"Do we need our coats outside?"	"Why don't you feel the window and find out."
"This is too heavy to move over to the sandbox."	"Do we have anything out here on the playground that will help you move it?"

"What do you want us to use to clean up all this water on the table?"

"Try this paper towel and a piece of paper and find out which works best."

"My hands are cold!"

"Try rubbing them together. How do they feel now?"

"Oh, I've dropped the straight pin on the carpet and can't find it!"

"Do we have anything on the science table that could help you find it?" (magnet)

"I can't get the styrofoam out from under the shelf."

"Do you think you could use the rhythm stick? Will blowing on it make it move?"

"The ball is in the mud puddle."

"What do you see that would help get it out without getting your feet wet?" (stick, broom, another ball, etc.)

When interacting with the children, use open-ended questions rather than ones that require only a yes or no answer. "What do we have that will reach the top shelf?" "Why do you think that happened?"

1

Bringing the Inside Out

SELF-EXPRESSION THROUGH ART

The purpose of art in the early childhood curriculum is to allow children to explore artistic media and to provide a vehicle for the creative expression of each individual child. Art is not imitation of the work of others (teacher's model), nor is it coloring inside the lines of a drawing. It is a process, not a product. It is often messy and incomplete by adult standards, but it is a representation of the child's world as he sees it and can express it.

The teacher's role is to establish an environment conducive to creativity. Provide the right materials, and have the right attitude. A variety of materials appropriate for the child's developmental level brings out the creative abilities that ALL children possess. Respect the work of each child; avoid comparisons and judgments. Every child's effort is valuable enough to be displayed. "Good" is not just those art works that appeal to the teacher.

Ask children to talk about their work. "Tell me about your picture" indicates interest in a child's work. "What is it?" might leave the child feeling inadequate with her artistic expression. A rich atmosphere and a caring and knowledgeable teacher are key components to the developing artist.

Using materials in a manner in which the limits are set only by the artistic media provided and the child's imagination will allow the children to express their own unique perception of the world and, therefore, to be creative.

....

This chapter offers open-ended activities in which each child can feel successful and where the process is valued more than the product. Experiences with a variety of art media and in a variety of art forms are provided with suggestions for extended application.

Confetti

- As children use hole punchers in other projects, have them save the punches. Separate by color and store in clear plastic jars.

- For an art activity, children draw designs with glue using an old paint brush, a dry marking pen or Q-tip.

- Children sprinkle color(s) of punches over glue designs.

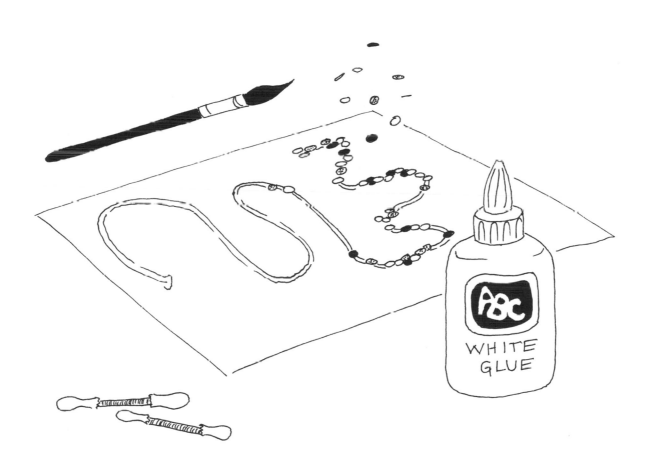

Tissue Paper Collage

- Provide children with cut pieces of tissue paper, liquid starch, brush and art paper.

- Children paint starch over paper and place tissue paper in a design of their choice.

Holiday Adaptation: For Valentine's Day, provide cut tissue paper hearts.

Pasta Art

- Provide a variety of uncooked pasta — macaroni, noodles, spaghetti, etc.

- Children glue pasta in designs on heavy art paper.

- Colorful additions can be made with crayon or markers.

Shades of Red

- Provide a red background for the collage. Provide many small bits of other red materials — red wrapping paper, red cloth, red feathers, red tissue paper, red ribbon, etc.

- Children create a monochromatic collage.

- Repeat on other days with other colors.

Flags and Pennants

- Provide children with pennant or flag shaped cutouts.

- Have available a variety of sizes and shapes of paper stars, stripes and circles for children to glue on flags or pennants.

- Tape to rolled up newspaper "stick."

Holiday Adaptation: Make a "bouquet" of flags to use on United Nations Day.

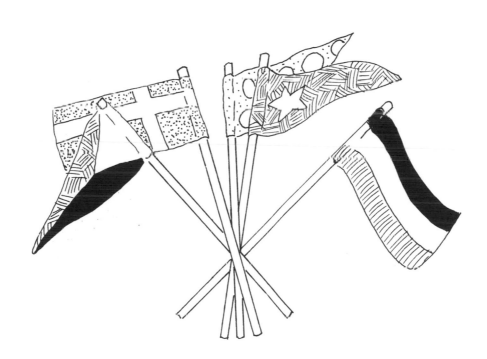

Leaf-on-Leaf

- Collect a variety of fall or spring leaves and let children glue on paper in designs of their choice.

- Or take children on a leaf walk and let them collect their own collage materials.

Humpty-Dumpties

- Save shells from boiled eggs.

- Break shells in small pieces.

- Shake shells in baggies with food coloring, or dye in a bowl with Easter egg dye.

- Pour on paper towels to dry.

- Children make collages by painting glue on art paper and sprinkling crushed egg shells on the glued area.

Holiday Adaptation: Using pastel coloring, many art projects associated with Easter are possible — for example, egg shell designs on large paper Easter eggs. This is a good after-Easter project when dyed shells are readily available.

Shape-on-Shape

- Cut one large circle (or square or triangle) from a grocery sack or butcher paper for each child.

- Cut a number of similar small shapes for each child.

- Children glue small circles on large circle (or small triangles on large triangle) in design of their choosing.

- Color can be added with crayons or markers.

Holiday Adaptation: Provide a large heart and numerous small hearts for Valentine's Day.

Patchworks

- Collect a variety of different textured, colored fabric pieces and cut them into usable sizes.

- Fabrics can be pre-classified according to prints (stripes, florals, etc.) or left unseparated.

- Children cover their papers with glue and then arrange the fabrics, creating their own design.

Box Collage

- Give each child, or a group of children, a large cardboard box.

- Let them cut out pictures and glue the pictures in collage fashion on the outside of the box.

- The box can be used for storage or turned over for use as a small table.

Glue Dots

- Use food coloring to tint two or three small containers of glue.

- Provide toothpicks for each color of glue.

- Children use toothpicks to dot glue on art paper in a free-form pattern, varying the colors they use.

Holiday Adaptation: Decorate a cut-out Christmas tree with various colored "balls."

Walking in the Rain

- Use blue food coloring to tint small containers of glue.

- Have children draw a picture and then dot over picture with toothpicks and glue, creating a falling rain scene.

Paper Towel Art

- Using food coloring, mix a number of different colors, each in a separate jar. Place an eyedropper in each jar.

- Place a paper towel or coffee filter on newspaper padding in a shallow pan.

- Let children use eyedroppers to drop color onto paper towels.

- As the color spots overlap, children will discover different colors.

Warming Tray Art

- Place a warming tray on low setting. Cover it with several sheets of newspaper to protect the children from the hot edges of the tray.

- Place a sheet of art paper on top of the newspaper and let the children take turns coloring with wax crayons. The children will discover a change in the "feel" of the way the crayon moves and a change in the "looks" of the drawing.

Follow That Car

- Secure felt markers of various colors to the back of toy cars using tape or rubber bands.

- Cover the floor with newspaper and place butcher paper on top of it.

- Children move the cars and trucks across the butcher paper, thus creating designs behind the moving car.

Straw Blowing

- Use a spoon to place a small amount of tempera paint on each child's paper.

- Give each child a straw (a cut-in-half straw is easier to handle).

- Allow children to blow through the straw to move paint across the paper and create a design.

Finger Paint Baggies

- Fill a large baggie with four tablespoons of finger paint. (Finger paint can be made by mixing tempera paint with liquid starch.)

- Place a baggie on the table in front of each child.

- Children create and re-create designs as they move their fingers over the top of the bag of paint.

Marble Painting

- Place a sheet of paper on a cookie sheet or inside a shallow cardboard box.

- Dip marbles into tempera paint.

- Place marbles on the cookie sheet or in the box and let children rotate the box to move the marbles around, thus creating a design.

✳ Golf balls can be used for a slightly different effect.

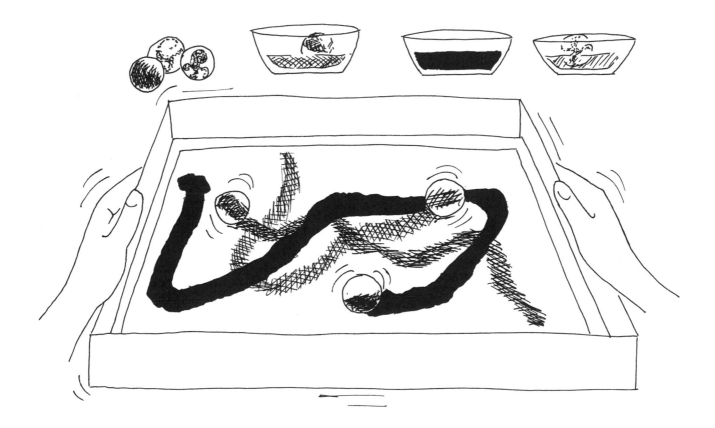

Spotted Leaves

- Collect large fall leaves.

- Provide children with Q-tips, thick tempera paint and a large leaf.

- Let children drop dots of color on leaves.

Circle Kites

- Provide each child with a circle (one foot in diameter) cut from a grocery sack.

- Let children glue thin streamers on the circle.

- When dry, punch two holes and insert a string.

- Children go outside and run with their circle kites while streamers ripple in the breeze.

- Or, a fan, placed in a safe location, can be used to "fly" a few kites at a time inside the room.

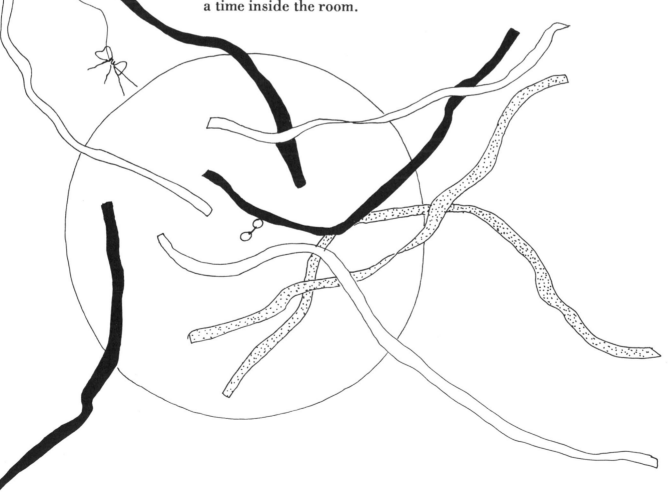

36

Crowns

- Make crowns for children by cutting out headbands from grocery sacks.

- Provide collage material to decorate the headbands — beads from old jewelry, feathers, ribbon bits, bits of shiny gift wrapping paper, etc.

Holiday Adaptations: Make Indian headbands for Thanksgiving, candle crowns for Christmas, heart crowns for Valentine's Day or flower crowns for May Day.

Big and Little Circles

- Provide children with art paper, masking tape rings, empty toilet tissue rolls, crayons and tempera paint poured on pads of folded paper towels.

- Children create designs by tracing the centers of masking tape rings to make big circles. To make small circles, children press ends of cardboard toilet tissue rolls on towels with paint and print small circles on paper.

Holiday Adaptations: Use red and green for Christmas, pink and light green for Easter or spring pictures.

Fish Bowl

- For each child, cut two wax paper fish bowls, one to be used as base for art and one to be used as top cover.

- Provide cut-out paper fish, green strips, small bits of white paper, blue circles, arched shapes, etc.

- Give children the base piece of wax paper, and have children arrange objects in a design of their choice and dot glue to base paper.

- Teacher irons the cover piece of wax paper over the design to seal in place.

Holiday Adaptation: Place red hearts in wax paper shapes and hang in the window for Valentine's Day.

My Hat

- Cut center out of paper plate and punch a hole on each side for ribbon ties.

- Provide each child with plate, tissue paper strips, giftwrap bows, etc.

- Have children dot glue on hat and decorate as they like.

- Place ribbons in the holes to tie the hat under the chin.

Holiday Adaptation: Make Easter hats and have an Easter Parade.

Tape Surprise

- Provide children with masking tape and art paper.

- Children tear the tape and stick it on paper.

- When the tape design is complete, children sponge over the design with paint.

- When the paint is nearly dry, children remove the tape to reveal a white design in the paint.

Shake-a-Color

- Provide several small baby food jars with lids and dry tempera paint.

- Children spoon coarse white sand into baby food jars. Teacher adds a little tempera to each jar, using different colors for each jar. Close tightly. Children shake the jars until the color spreads throughout sand.

- Pour colored sand into an empty baby food jar or salad dressing bottle in alternating color patterns.

Holiday Adaptations: Each child prepares a jar of variegated sand for Mother's Day, Father's Day or Christmas gift. Add a bow for decoration.

TEMPERA

RED

Banners

- Using poster paper, make long strips three inches wide and two to three feet long for children to use as background.

- Let children draw tall designs, many small designs, or paste a variety of cutouts on the background strips.

- Hang in the window like vertical venetian blinds.

Holiday Adaptations: Paste on pumpkins and bats for Halloween, hearts for Valentine's Day and Easter eggs for Easter.

41

Winter Pictures

- Have children draw a winter background scene — a bare tree, a snowman or a landscape.

- Provide white styrofoam packing material and glue.

- Children glue styrofoam chips onto their winter scene.

Rough Stuff

- Provide children with a selection of granular-type substances, such as salt, sand, coffee grounds, etc.

- Children paint glue on heavy art paper and sprinkle substances in desired area of design.

Holiday Adaptations: Dye rice with food coloring for appropriate holiday collages — orange for Halloween pumpkin, various colors for Christmas balls, red for Valentine's hearts, pale colors for Easter eggs.

Party Hats

- Make each child a newspaper hat.

- Provide paper feathers, real feathers, geometric paper shapes and other collage items to glue on hats.

Holiday Adaptation: Have a Fourth of July parade.

Wood Sculpting

- Obtain small pieces of lumber from a lumber store or through parent request list.

- Provide glue and let children arrange and glue pieces together, creating their own designs.

Box Sculpting

- Provide boxes of varying sizes, from the size of small jewelry boxes to the size of shoe boxes.

- Children glue boxes together and on top of each other, creating their own unique configurations.

✶ Small bits of cloth and various bits of ribbon may also be provided to add additional design interest.

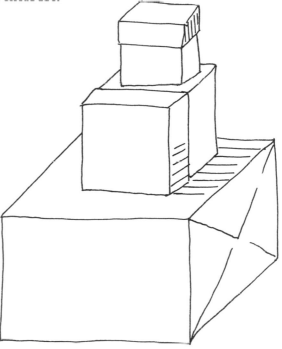

Stabiles

- Provide each child with a drinking cup lid, pipe cleaners, playdough (or modeling clay) and objects cut out from greeting cards (or small magazine pictures).

- Children glue cutouts on one end of the pipe cleaner. The other end of the pipe cleaner is inserted in the playdough which has been placed on the cup lid.

- Children arrange several pipe cleaners on cup lids at various heights and twisted in different shapes.

✳ Stabile lid may be placed in a small box to display it.

Holiday Adaptations: Use Christmas card cutouts for Christmas, hearts for Valentine's Day and eggs for Easter.

Flower Arranging

- Place clay or used floral styrofoam in the bottom of a small box or basket. Secure to bottom of container.

- Provide a variety of plastic or silk flowers and greenery.

- Children arrange and re-arrange flowers in floral designs of their choosing.

Balls, Ropes, Beads and Bracelets

- Mix playdough, using recipe below: (Playdough recipe #1)

- When cool, place in covered containers or plastic bag.

- Children use and re-use playdough, molding it into shapes of their choice.

Playdough Recipe #1

1 Cup flour   1/2 Cup salt

1 Cup boiling water   1 Tablespoon alum

1 Tablespoon cooking oil

Dissolve alum in oil and water. Mix flour and salt and add to water mixture. Knead when cool.

Biscuits

- Using the recipe below, or Recipe #1, prepare playdough for children's use.

- Provide rolling pins for rolling the dough and stocking egg halves and thimbles for cutting the biscuits.

Playdough Recipe #2

1 Cup flour   1/2 Cup salt

1 Cup water   1 Tablespoon vegetable oil

2 teaspoons cream of tartar

Heat ingredients until they form a ball. Knead after mixture cools. Mixture can be stored in covered container for use and re-use.

Holiday Adaptations: Add food coloring to water for holiday colors: green and red for Christmas, red for Valentine's Day, pastels for Easter and orange for Halloween.

Sand Castles

- On a warm, sunny summer day, moisten the sand in the sandbox to the consistency of beach sand.

- Let children put on bathing suits and make sand castles.

- Provide disposable cups and sticks for shaping the castle.

- Provide leaves and twigs for landscaping if desired.

✽ Have a water hose ready to rinse off the sand castle builders when they are finished.

Mud Sculpting

- For summer water play (when children are in bathing suits), place pans of water in the sandbox so children can mix sand and water to make mud pies.

- Place a tire, or other smooth surface, in the sandbox to use as a display table for "cookies," "pies" and other sculpted creations.

Stained Glass Windows

- Prepare a thick tempera paint with detergent, and provide children with small paint brushes and paint.

- Cover the wall and floor area with newspaper for protection.

- Define a space for each child on the window with masking tape, and allow children to take turns painting directly on the window inside the area defined by tape.

- Remove tape when all the painting is done and fill in the tape lines with dark paint.

The Shape's The Thing

- For a variation at the easel, cut the easel paper into different shapes — a square, a circle or an ellipse.

Holiday Adaptations: Valentine's Day — cut into heart shapes; Easter — cut into giant egg shapes; Christmas — cut tree shapes.

Vanishing Art

- Provide paint brushes and small plastic buckets of water for children to paint on the easel.

- Children will also discover the principles of evaporation.

Touchy Paint

- Add sharp sand or granular detergent to paint to create a different effect.

Deodorant Bottle Painting

- Mix tempera paint to a thick consistency.

- Remove tops of roll-on deodorant bottles. Pour paint in bottles. Replace roll-on tops.

- Children roll paint on art paper, creating their own designs.

Little Wall Painters

- Obtain several used, small wall painting roller brushes (the edger type).

- Children can paint at the easel or on a wall protected by plastic and covered with art paper.

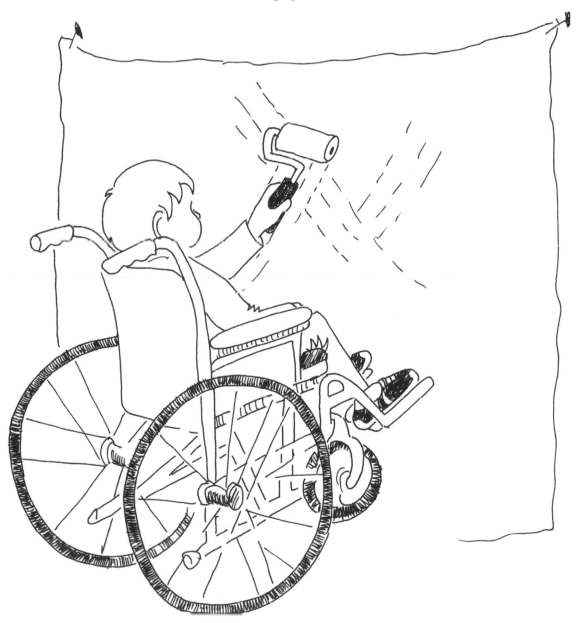

Purple Passion

- Provide each child with red and blue finger paint.

- Let them discover the creation of a new color (purple) by blending red and blue as they finger paint.

Holiday Adaptations: Provide red and yellow for children to discover orange as they draw pumpkins. Provide red and white, blue and white, green and white for children to discover pastel shades for spring or Easter.

Double Take

- Add granular detergent to finger paint.

- After children have drawn designs with their fingers, place another piece of art paper over the drawings. Pat lightly. Lift the second sheet. The finger paint design will be duplicated on the second sheet.

Speedy

- If commercial finger paint is not available, spread liquid starch on art paper. Sprinkle dry tempera on the starch. As children work the starch and tempera together with their finger(s), a finger paint consistency develops.

- Finger painting can also be done on a cookie sheet.

Cooked Homemade Finger Paint

- Teacher can prepare homemade finger paint using the following recipe:

4 Cups of cold water

6 teaspoons of cornstarch

Mix a small amount of cold water with cornstarch until smooth. Gradually add the remainder of the water. Cook the mixture over low heat until it is clear and the consistency of pudding. Add tempera for color.

- When cool, spoon on art paper or pan for finger painting fun.

Spool Printing

- Prepare several colors of tempera paint and pour each color on a sponge.

- Using old thread spools, children place a spool on a color sponge and print on art paper.

- Designs may be made with one or all the colors provided.

Fingerprint Art

- Pour tempera paint onto a paper towel that has been placed on a plate.

- Child presses her finger on the paint pad and then creates a design on butcher paper.

- Depending on colors provided, children can print oranges or lemons on a tree, scales on a fish, feathers on an owl, etc.

Holiday Adaptation: Provide a variety of colors for decorating a Christmas tree.

Fold-Over I

- Give children a folded piece of construction paper.

- Have them paint only on one side.

- While the paint is still wet fold the other side over the picture. Rub your hands on the outside, then open to reveal a duplicated picture.

Fold-Over II

- Give children a cut-out butterfly shape, which has been folded.

- Prepare paint in a thick consistency.

- Children dot color on one wing, or paint the wing entirely with a variety of colors.

- Fold other wing over and rub. Colors will blend as they are reproduced on top wing.

- Display butterflies on dry limb anchored in a bucket of sand.

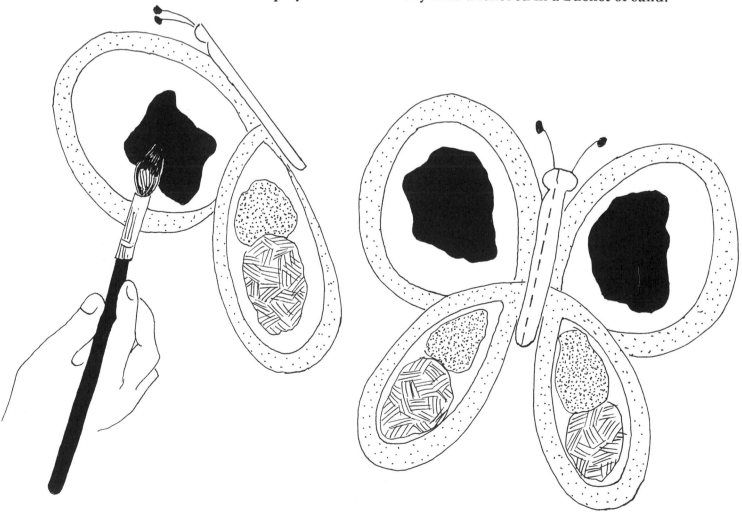

Sponge Prints

- Cut sponges in a variety of shapes.

- Prepare tempera paint and pour a thin layer into a flat dish.

- Children dip sponges in the paint and print designs on butcher paper.

Holiday Adaptation: Use printed paper to wrap Christmas gifts.

Hand Mural

- Prepare tempera paints of different colors and pour on folded paper towels in pie pans.

- Children press hands on towel of tempera and print on large sheet of butcher paper hanging on wall. Hands can overlap in design of choice.

- Have rinse bucket and towel ready for painted hands.

Car Tracks

- Pour tempera paint over a sponge (or paper towel). Prepare a different color for each sponge.

- Place small cars by each color of prepared tempera.

- Children roll cars across tempera soaked sponge and then roll on art paper to create a colored track design which can lap and overlap.

Gadget Painting

- Prepare tempera paint and pour it on a paper towel "sponge."

- Provide children with several objects that can be pressed on the color soaked towel and printed on art paper — kitchen whisk, fork, potato masher, etc.

Shape Surprises

- Cut a variety of cardboard shapes.

- Children place shapes under their art paper.

- Using the sides of their crayons, children "rub" (color) all over the paper, revealing the shapes underneath.

  Holiday Adaptations: Provide tree cutouts for Christmas, hearts for Valentine's Day and shamrocks for St. Patrick's Day.

Rub and Color

- Provide a limited number of large cardboard cut-out shapes, such as a diamond, a square, a circle, a rectangle, etc.

- After children have made rubbings, let them turn the shapes into other designs by coloring with crayons.

  Examples: diamonds to kites by adding string

  square to table by adding legs

  circle to face by adding eyes, mouth, nose

  rectangle to a window by adding lines to create window panes

Meat Tray Art

- Provide each child with a styrofoam meat tray and crayons.

- Children draw directly on the trays.

- Punch two holes in top; insert strip of yarn to make a hanger.

Holiday Adaptations: This can make a nice Mother's Day, Father's Day or Christmas gift.

Good Graffiti

- On days when the ground is soggy and when children can't play on grass, give them chalk to draw on the sidewalk or patio.

Sugar Water Drawing

- Give each child a small baby food jar.

- Put three tablespoons of sugar in each jar, and add enough lukewarm water to fill the jar.

- Shake the jar until the sugar is dissolved. When the water becomes clear, question the disappearance of the sugar.

- Pour the sugar water into bowls. Provide each child with colored chalk. Children draw pictures by dipping the chalk in sugar water.

- When dry, the pictures will sparkle with crystallized sugar.

Buttermilk Drawings

- Sponge over art paper with a thin layer of buttermilk.

- Let children draw with colored chalk in design of their choosing, creating a thick, smooth, chalky drawing.

Classwork Quilt

- Provide art paper of the same size to each child.

- Have each child draw a picture on the art paper.

- When all the children have finished, arrange the pictures as quilt squares in a quilt.

- When the desired pattern is arranged, turn the pictures over and tape together on the back.

- Hang the "quilt" on the wall.

Table Design

- Make a tablecloth for the table by covering with butcher paper and taping down.

- Let children stand around the table and color with crayons.

- Music can be played while children are coloring.

Mini-Storage

- Cut the bottom half of clean bleach bottles down to three to five inches in height.

- Let children decorate with colored marking pens.

- Use for decorative storage boxes for crayons, swabs, stir-sticks and other art shelf items.

Holiday Adaptation: Fill with sand and place small flags in the sand for the Fourth of July.

Wet Sand Drawing

- Before outdoor play time, water the sand in the sandbox.

- Children group around the perimeter of the sandbox, leaning into the sandbox and making designs in the sand with sticks, combs and potato mashers.

- Provide a watering can for children to re-moisten the sand when needed.

Wash Overs

- Give children wax crayons and paper to draw designs of their choice.

- After completing their drawing, children wash over the design by sponging with tempera paint, covering the entire paper.

Holiday Adaptations: For Valentine's Day have children draw hearts with red crayons and sponge with pink tempera paint; for Halloween, draw with black and sponge with orange.

Mega-Pix

- Using grocery sacks or butcher paper, cut large shapes for each child — circle, rectangle, star, etc.

- Children draw a design on the paper and wash over it by sponging with tempera paint.

Holiday Adaptations: With appropriate color of paint and design shape, children can make a large egg for Easter or a tree for Christmas.

Big and Wide

- Provide a large piece of paper that is at least four feet wide.

- Let children color, paint, print or draw on the mural paper and then hang it on the wall.

How Does Your Garden Grow?

- Provide children with long strips of green for flower stalks and short pieces of green for leaves. Let them cut the pieces to the length and shape they want. Glue on the mural paper, leaving space for flowers.

- Prepare several small cups of food coloring mixed with water.

- To make flowers, children use eyedroppers to dot colored water on coffee filters. When dry, coffee filter flowers are glued on stems.

Art Hints for Teachers

- **Parent Request Lists:**

  Many items for art projects can be obtained by informing parents of the need. From their home or office, parents can supply items that might otherwise be thrown away, for example, computer paper (good art paper), bleach bottles, grocery sacks, old paint rollers, manila folders (good backgrounds for heavy collage), meat trays, etc.

  By requesting and accepting re-usable items, the teacher helps parents feel involved with their children's educational process.

- **Matting Pictures:**

  Glue pictures on squares of wallpaper (from wallpaper sample book) or on newspaper.

- **Framing Pictures:**

  Cut a picture size square out of one side of a manilla folder or brown mailing envelope. Insert picture. Can be used and re-used. Cut two inch wide strips of construction paper and glue around the four edges of art work.

- **Name Savers:**

  Write child's name in wax crayon on easel paper before child paints — a functional use for crayon resist.

- **Glue Stretchers:**

  Add water to white glue, stir and mix. Buy in bulk and keep in small containers. Dip a wet sponge in a dish of glue and let children rub their item to be glued over the sponge.

2

The Magic of Make Believe

DRAMATIC PLAY AND IMAGINATION

Dramatic Play and Imagination

Dramatic play has many advantages for the young child. It allows children to assume roles (become big people who control or babies who need more attention), to clarify life situations by acting them out, to express feelings in a safe and acceptable environment and to reconcile the two worlds of fantasy and reality. Imagination is an important component of the developmental process. It allows children to be creative, to use problem-solving techniques, to project consequences, to arrange situations, to adapt to unplanned events, to negotiate and to work within situational limits. All of these elements develop scientific thinking, interpersonal skills and full intellectual potential.

A safe and interesting environment for dramatic play, including both the classroom and playground, provides appropriate opportunities. The homemaking center is an obvious area to create dramatic play situations. However, the block center, the sand box, the fort and other play areas outside are also perfect set-ups for situational development and use of imagination. Large blocks of time are necessary so that play can develop fully.

The role of the teacher is one of unobtrusive observer. The direct flow of dramatic developments should be uninterrupted unless problems are arising or the direction of the activity is moving to unacceptable behaviors. It takes real skill on the part of the teacher to know how to intercede without controlling the dramatic play situation. The teacher needs to be available for temporary interaction, but must not become an unwanted participant in the play itself.

Rotate the materials in the learning center, and provide opportunities for both boys and girls to participate. Props for housekeeping can be changed to props for a store, post office, pizza parlor, doctor's office and flower shop. Briefcases, lunch kits and firefighter's hats should be available, as well as purses, pots and pans and bridal veils.

Beyond the learning center, teachers can plan activities that stimulate dramatic play. Dramatizing *Goldilocks and the Three Bears,* walking to "giant" music or making grass skirts are examples of these activities. Transitions provide a further opportunity for dramatic play. Moving from one room to another like bunnies, butterflies or elephants provides an interesting way to achieve an objective and have fun doing it.

This chapter includes activities that suggest ways to set the stage for dramatic play. Ideas for learning centers, group interaction and transitions are provided.

During the early years children are just beginning to form concepts and understand the skills necessary for successful social interaction. Dramatic play situations greatly enhance the formation of these skills, but are dependent on a teacher who understands the value of dramatic play to the social, emotional and cognitive development of the young child.

Car Wash

- On a water play day, hook up the hose and let children wash cars (wheeled toys).

- Provide buckets of mild soap and rags for washing.

- Provide large rags or towels for drying.

Gas Station

- Set up a semi-permanent gas station on the playground.

- Attach an old hose to a post for use as a gas hose, and use other hoses for air and water. Label.

- Place a "tool box" near the gas station, with toy tools. Tool box could be portable for storage after a day of use.

Tent Town

- On hot sunny days, create shade by making sheet tents.

- Clip a bed sheet (or other large pieces of fabric) to the fence with clothespins.

- Secure the opposite end of the sheet by placing the end under the picnic table legs or placing tires on the edges of the sheet.

- An alternate method is to clip the sheet to the fence and tie the opposite corners of the sheet to a tree or a piece of playground equipment.

- If several tents are "built," dramatic play will develop in many ways.

Drive-In

- Obtain a large appliance box.

- Cut a door and a window in the box.

- Place the box in the play yard near the wheeled toy path so children can drive-in to order.

- Use styrofoam boxes for "take-out" orders. Stack on a small table placed in the box.

- Provide a cap for the "clerk."

- One child at a time can go in the box and serve the "customers" as they drive by.

Ship Ahoy

- Obtain a small rowboat that is no longer used in the water.

- Place in the play yard and stabilize so that the boat is level and doesn't rock. (This can be done by placing it in a small trench and/or placing sand or sandbags around the sides.)

- Children "drive" the boat or "fish" at will.

✳ The boat may become a permanent or temporary addition to the playground equipment.

School Crossing Guard

- Prepare a hand held **STOP** sign, using cardboard and paint.

- Provide a cape and cap.

- Children take turns being a crossing guard on the playground.

Little Designers

- In the dramatic play area, place a variety of male and female dress-up clothes, for example, hats, caps, scarves, flowers, belts, ties, costume jewelry, purses, briefcases and lunch kits.

- Also provide a mirror, full-length if available.

- Schedule time for children to explore all the possible combinations of items until a pleasurable product is developed. The final form may vary a number of times.

- Be sure to have a multicultural variety of clothes, such as dashikis, ponchos, saris, kimonos, parkas, etc.

Block Center Additions

- Include other items in the block center so that play may be extended, for example, small cars and trucks, ramps and pulleys, little plastic or wooden people, cardboard tubes for tunnels, small stop sign and other road signals, etc.

Flowers, Flowers Everywhere

- Provide plastic, paper or cloth flowers and greenery.

- Place styrofoam bases in each of several vases or baskets. Secure to bottom with clay.

- Children arrange floral pieces in designs of their choosing. Place arrangements around the room or in homemaking center.

Holiday Adaptation: Use real flowers for May Day presentations.

Eat Your Dinner, Please

- Place a tablecloth on the homemaking center table.

- Provide dishes and silverware for setting the table.

- Also provide a variety of food pictures which have been cut from magazines and glued to cardboard backing.

- Scene is set for a re-play of children's experiences with meal time.

Bathtime for Baby

- Cover a table with towels.

- Place a baby tub partially filled with water on the table.

- Provide washable dolls, extra towels, wash cloths and mild soap.

- Let children bathe babies and redress them.

The Nursery

- Provide a rocking chair, diaper bag, stroller, baby bed, baby carrier, blankets, dolls and doll clothes for children in the dramatic play center.

- Be sure to let both boys and girls participate in nurturing activities.

Box House

- Obtain a large appliance box to use as a playhouse.

- Cut doors and windows in it.

- Tape curtains on the windows and glue flowers on the outside.

- Children may also choose to paint the outside of the house.

- Children create situations as they play with the house.

Dress-up Parade

- Plan a day in which children can dress up as mommies and daddies. Ask parents for cooperation in preparing outfits so children can walk safely. (No high heels, no dresses too long to step on.)

- Allow children to push baby carriages, carry briefcases and lunch kits, etc.

- Parade around the school grounds or around the neighborhood.

Holiday Adaptation: Have a Halloween parade in the neighborhood.

Office Prop Box

- Prepare a prop box that can be brought into the classroom from time to time to simulate an office.

- Include items such as an old typewriter or computer, various pads of paper, tape dispensers, telephone, stack boxes, briefcases, eyeglass frames, etc.

- Place in an area with small tables and chairs that children can arrange as they choose.

* Involve parents in preparing this prop box so that children might have identifiable items from their parents' workplaces.

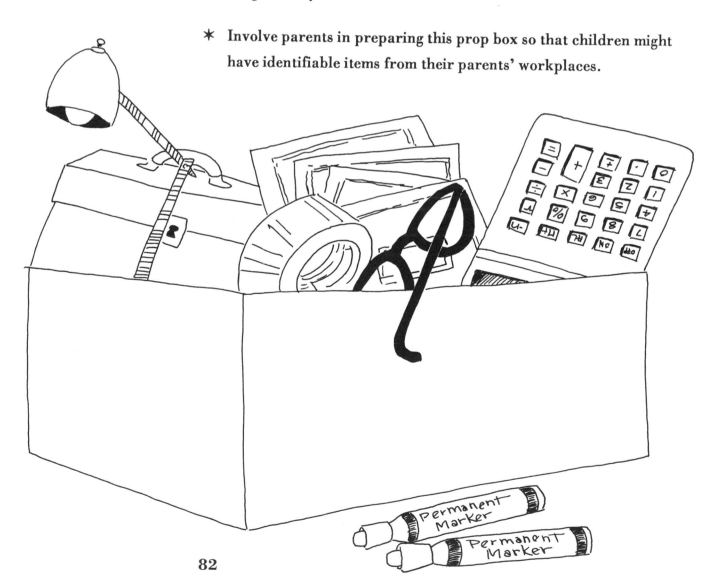

82

Circus Prop Box

- Prepare a Circus Prop Box that can be brought into the classroom from time to time to simulate a circus.

- Include such items as clown costumes, ballet shoes, ballet costumes, wigs, a small umbrella, a round plastic tub, yarn on the end of a straw to stimulate animal tamer, etc.

- Ask children to bring stuffed circus animals for the week that the prop box is in use.

- Set up in an area where chairs can be arranged for an audience and a masking tape line can be put on the floor for a tightrope.

Beauty Parlor Prop Box

- Prepare a Beauty Parlor Prop Box that can be brought into the classroom from time to time to simulate a beauty parlor.

- Include items such as hairdryers (with cord cut), plastic rollers, combs (sterilized), empty spray bottles, telephone, calendar, pencils, magazines, etc.

- Place in an area where children can have use of several chairs and a table (for receptionist).

Hat Prop Box

- Collect a variety of headwear. Assemble in a prop box.

- Include pictures of individuals wearing similar headwear. Examples: berets, military hats, turbans, parka hoods, sombreros, straw hats, kerchiefs, babushkas, cowboy hats, fezzes, gaucho hats, conductor's hats, firehats, etc.

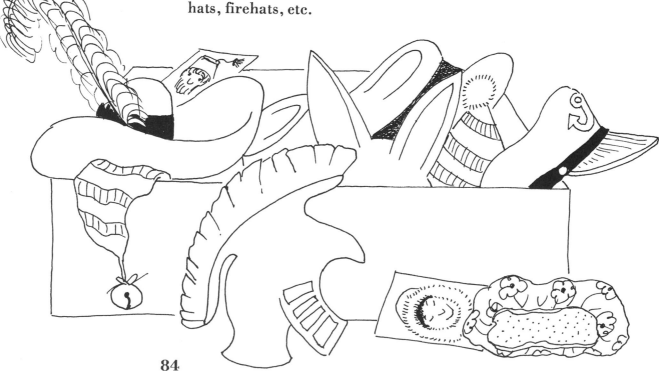

84

Baubles, Beads, Bangles and Belts

- Provide colored macaroni, cardboard tubes, old beads, styrofoam bits, scarf clips, old belt buckles, cut straws or other stringable items.

- Cut a necklace (or belt) length of yarn or string. Tie a large knot at one end, and prepare the other end for inserting into decorative items. Dip this end in glue (and dry), or wrap masking tape around it.

- Children design and string materials in arrangements as they desire. Can be used as a belt or a necklace for dress-up.

Mad Hatters

- Provide a variety of baskets, ribbons, flowers and beads.

- Encourage children to invert baskets, decorate and make hats.

- Childrens' interest may be stimulated by reading *Jennie's Hat* by Ezra Jack Keats.

Jack and Bo-Peep

- Make a pretend candle with a toilet tissue roll and yellow tissue paper. Let a few children jump over the candlestick to interpret "Jack, Be Nimble, Jack Be Quick, Jack Jump Over the Candlestick."

- The rest of the group guesses which nursery rhyme is being demonstrated.

- Continue with "Little Jack Horner" and a pretend pie; "Little Bo Peep" and her lost sheep, etc.

Billy Goats Gruff

- Make a masking tape bridge on the floor. Teacher tells the story of *The Three Billy Goats Gruff* as three children act out the goats walking over the bridge and another child acts out the troll under the bridge.

- Let children take turns acting out the parts.

Goldilocks

- Tell the story of *Goldilocks and the Three Bears.*

- After telling the story, place three bowls on table, three chairs against wall and three sheets on the floor (representing beds).

- Retell the story, letting children take the part of the bears and Goldilocks.

- Let children insert their own dialogue at the critical points of "It's too hot!" "It's too cold!" "This is just right," etc.

Pantomime Stories

- Read a story, such as *The Snowy Day* by Ezra Jack Keats.

- Let one, or several children, pantomime the activity of the lead character as he looks for the snowball in his pocket, makes angels in the snow, etc.

- Tell the story again and let another child, or a few children, interpret the story as he visualizes the actions.

Where Am I?

- As children are completing clean-up tasks and are gathering for circle, ask them to pretend they are in the library. Teacher may provide a book as a prop.

- Other environments for quiet waiting periods include sitting at the lake fishing, in the nursery rocking a baby and sitting at a desk typing.

Who Am I?

- As children leave circle and go outside for play, have a few leave as tightrope walkers, others as horseriders and still others as Indians, clowns, basketball players and toddlers.

What Is It?

- Place a sheet on the wall or use a movie screen.

- Create a light source by using a high intensity lamp or projector light.

- Using your hands in between the light source and the screen, make shadows on the screen with your hands and let children describe what they "see."

Dancing
Shadows

- Place a sheet on the wall or use a movie screen.

- Create a light source by using a high intensity lamp or projector light.

- While playing a record, let children take turns interpreting the movements of a particular animal (bird, kangaroo, lion, etc.) while dancing in front of the light source.

- Class tries to identify the animal.

Cloud Watch

- On a cloudy day, when the sun is in a location that won't be directly in children's eyes, take the class outside.

- Have everyone lie down on their backs, on a towel or sheet.

- Ask each child to look at the clouds and describe the shapes seen (shapes could include camels, castles, snowmen, etc.).

- Suggestions are limited only by children's imaginations.

Torn Paper Silhouettes

- Provide each child with a large shape that has been randomly torn from light colored paper.

- Children paste the shape on darker background art paper.

- With crayons and imagination, children turn the shape into a picture.

Toast Tid-bits

- When children are having toast for snack or breakfast, the teacher can informally stimulate children's imaginations by commenting on the shape of the toast after bitting into it.

  Example: "My toast looks like a tree."

  "Leroy, what does yours look like?"

  "Lisa Marie, try turning your toast the other way."

- Children can continue biting their toast in different places to create imaginary shapes.

- All suggestions are accepted.

Inch by Inch

- Collect a variety of interesting magazine pictures.

- Place each picture inside a manila folder.

- Pull each picture out of its folder, revealing parts of the picture a little at a time.

- Let children guess what the picture is.

- When guessing is over, reveal the whole picture and discuss.

Color House

- To create a private space for a child, obtain a large appliance box.

- Cut an opening in the top of the box. Make cellophane panels of different colors to fit this opening.

- Place the box in a lighted area.

- Child crawls in and discovers the effect of color on the outside world.

- Change the color panels when appropriate.

✳ To create a space ship, use a box big enough for two.

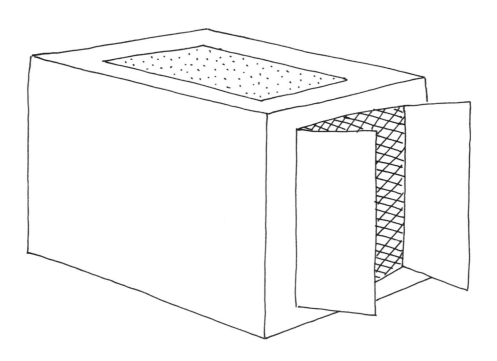

Imagination Chair

- Decorate a special chair to be called the "Imagination Chair." It could be an adult sized chair with a pretty cushion and bows.

- Children take turns sitting in the chair and describing what they would do if they were a certain person of importance or renown.

    Examples: "If I were a king (or queen), I would..."

    "If I were an astronaut, I would..."

Holiday Adaptation: "If I were Santa Claus, I would..."

Box Cars and Boats

- At various times, bring medium to large size boxes into the room for children to use as they wish. Boxes should be big enough for children to sit in.

- A one-child box might become a car, and a long box might become a canoe for two.

- Children might place a series of boxes in a line to make a train.

Sheet Castles

- Drape a sheet over several chairs to create a play house or tent in the room.

- Let children's imaginations embellish and furnish the "castles."

Groovy Moves

- As children go from a large group activity to an individual activity, have them demonstrate a way to move other than on their feet, for example, crawl on hands and knees, scoot on seat, roll or wiggle like a worm, etc.

Weather Walks

- As children move as a group, or individually, have them demonstrate how they would walk in a strong wind, on a hot day, in a snow storm or in a flood.

Butterfly Flutter

- As children move from the classroom down the halls, have them pretend to be butterflies.

- **Before beginning, ask the children if a butterfly makes any noise. Let several children demonstrate their interpretation of how a butterfly moves before the group starts.**

- Other suggested animal movements are elephants, cats, mice and spiders.

Wacky Walk

- As children move from a group activity to individual activities, have them demonstrate how they would walk on any of the following surfaces:

caramel candy	syrup
hot tin roof	mud
cotton	marshmallows
tall field of grass	

3

Basic Builders for Muscle Mastery

FINE AND GROSS MOTOR SKILLS

Fine and Gross Motor Skills

Fine motor activities develop the small muscles of the hand and enable children to develop competence in manipulating materials in their environment and, ultimately, to master the skill of writing in the primary school years.

Materials, equipment and activities that require the child to manipulate with his fingers and hands, make precise movements and use dexterity will develop the small muscles of the hand. Puzzles, string beads, interlocking toys and playdough are examples of these materials. All cutting, coloring, drawing and folding activities will contribute to competence in this area. Cleaning tables with sponges, playing with sand, folding napkins, buttoning coats and lacing shoes are routine activities that also contribute to fine motor development.

Gross motor activities develop the large muscles of the body, the arms, legs and torso, and enable children to develop mastery of body movements. As children develop mastery over their bodies, their self-esteem increases. Early experiences with gross motor activities lay a foundation for a lifetime commitment to physical fitness.

In order to develop their large muscles, children need balls to throw, ropes to jump and climb, tricycles to ride, wagons to pull, as well as swings, slides and climbing apparatus. Activities like marching, scarf waving, bending, bowing and dancing all contribute to the development of the whole body. The playground is a major component of the gross motor development program, providing space for children to run and play.

A playground with space and equipment and a classroom with developmentally appropriate materials will provide the setting for children to develop their fine and gross motor skills. This chapter describes activities that encourage the development of the child's mastery of her body. Through movement of the body and manipulation of materials the child is also learning spatial concepts and developing hand-eye coordination. Fine and gross motor skill development is an important component of the early childhood curriculum.

Liquid Movers

- Give the children a tub of water and a variety of objects that pick up water, such as basters, syringes and eyedroppers.

- Let the children experiment with each item. They can use tally marks to record how many times each item must be used to fill up an eight ounce cup.

Twisted Sculpture

- Give children pipe cleaners or telephone wire.

- Children twist the pipe cleaners or telephone wire into any shape they desire.

- Let each child describe his sculpture to his friends.

✴ Wires can be placed in a small amount of modeling clay to make the sculpture free standing.

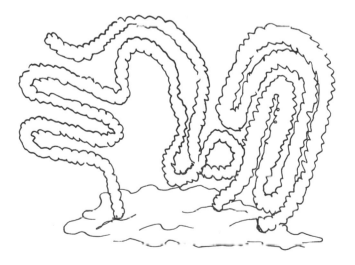

Easy Cutouts

- Give each child several pages from a magazine.

- Circle some items on each page.

- Let the children cut out the items by cutting around the circles the teacher has drawn. This is easier and less frustrating than cutting around intricate details.

Nut Sorting

- Provide children with several types of nuts in shells, such as pecans, walnuts and almonds, tongs and a muffin tin.

- Children pick up nuts with the tongs and transfer them to the muffin pan.

Seed Sorting

- Provide children with several types of seeds, for example, pumpkin, popcorn and apple, tweezers and a muffin tin.

- Children pick up seeds with tweezers and sort into the muffin tin.

Punch Me Out

- Provide each child with a small design cut from white paper.

- Let children punch holes in the cutouts with hole punchers.

- Punched shape(s) can then be pasted on a colored background paper to create an artistic design.

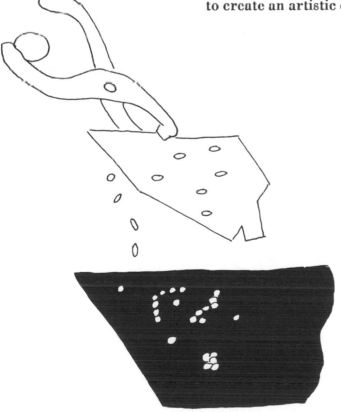

Fish Kites

- Provide each child with a cut-out fish shape, folded in half.

- Draw cut lines on each fish (lines are drawn from fold toward outer edge of fish but not to the edge).

- Children cut on cut lines.

- Open the fish and tape to a string for children to run with on playground.

- Children with well-developed cutting skills can do the complete process, using a pattern to make fish.

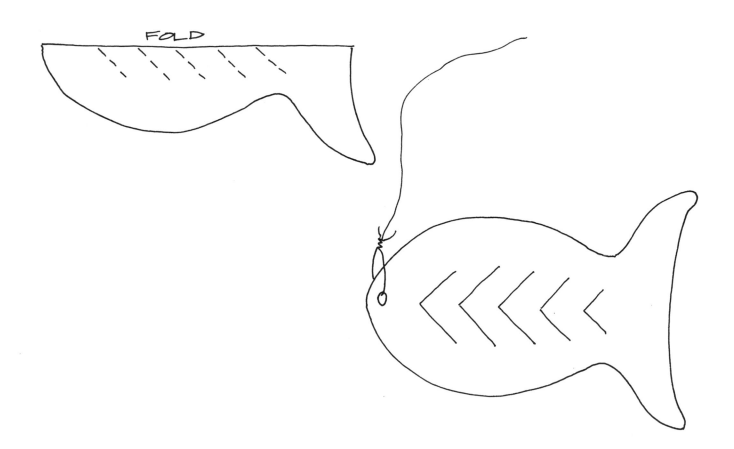

Table Top Finger Painting

- Place finger paint directly onto the top of a table.

- Let children create designs directly on the table top.

- The design can be transferred onto a sheet of paper by placing the paper face down over the design, smoothing the back side with your hand and then lifting up.

Water Transfer

- Place a sponge and a clear plastic glass or pill canister on a styrofoam meat tray.

- Children use an eyedropper to transfer water from the glass to the sponge.

- The sponge can then be pressed and water will be released into the tray. The water can be transferred, using the eyedropper, from the tray back into the glass.

✱ Food coloring in the water may be added to create interest.

Clay Letters

- Fill an old cookie sheet with a thin layer of modeling clay.

- Let children use a pencil or stick to draw letters or designs.

- When designs are complete, the children use their fingers to press the letters or designs out of the clay. This provides additional exercise to strengthen the muscles.

Shaving Cream Designs

- Spray a table top with shaving cream.

- Children write their names or create designs directly on the table top.

* This activity makes clean up and erasing mistakes easy.

Tracing

- Write familiar vocabulary words on five by seven inch index cards. Use a bold print and correct manuscript form.

- Cover the card with onion skin paper, using a paper clip to secure the paper to the card.

- Provide large pencils or crayons.

- Children trace the words. Line drawings from coloring books may also be used for tracing experiences.

Sand Drawing

- Cover a cookie sheet with sand, salt or cornmeal.

- Children create designs using their fingers.

- Word or design cards may be used for examples of letters or patterns.

Tracing Lids

- Provide a variety of sizes of plastic lids for children to trace around with crayons.

- Provide lids in which geometric shapes have been cut. Children place the lids on background paper. Using crayons, children trace the shape inside the lid.

Cookie Cutter Trace

- Provide a variety of cookie cutters for children to trace around with crayons.

- Children can add other designs to traced shapes.

Holiday Adaptations: Use seasonal cookie cutters, for example, Christmas tree, hearts, pumpkins, etc.

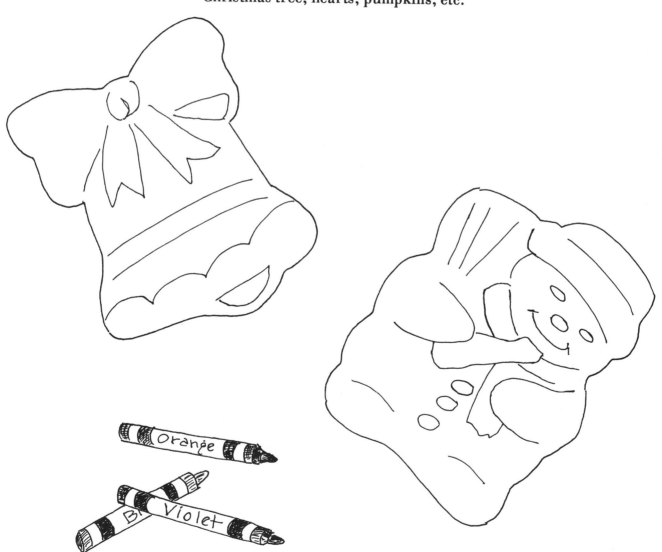

Squirt Bottle Painting

- Prepare several bottles of thick (consistency of mustard) tempera paint in plastic squirt bottles. Each bottle of paint should contain a different color.

- Children squirt colors on art paper to create designs.

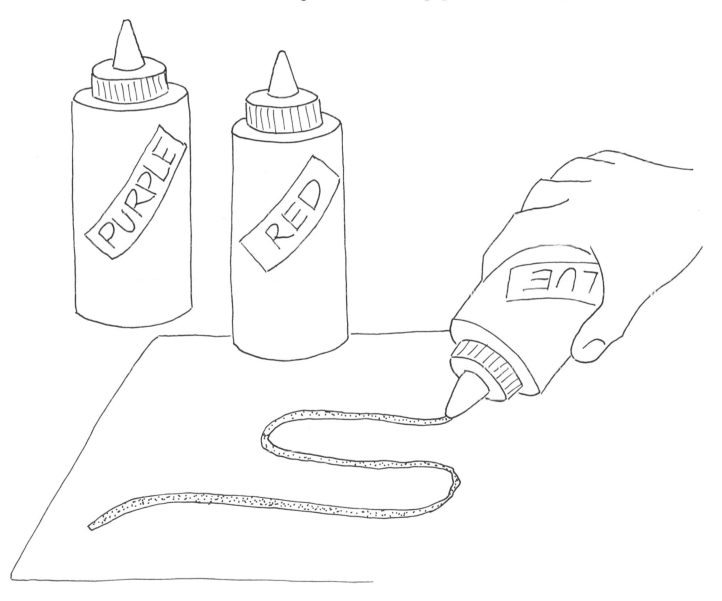

Cups of Color

- Fill all the cups of a muffin tin with water.

- Place red, blue, green and yellow food coloring in each of four of the cups of water.

- Children use eyedroppers to transfer colored water to other cups, thus creating different shades of color.

- By combining colors, children also create new colors of purple, chartreuse, brown, etc.

Macaroni Necklaces

- Provide large pieces of macaroni that have been dyed a variety of colors with food coloring.

- Children string macaroni on a strong cord or shoe lace to make necklaces.

Little Ships

- Provide a pan of water, tongs (or meatball press) and a bowl of styrofoam chips.

- Children transfer styrofoam chips from the bowl to pan of water.

- If a water table is available, several children can use tongs and "float ships" in the water table.

Bean Transfer

- Provide children with tweezers and dried beans in a cup.

- Give the children a butter tub with a lid for a receptacle for the beans. Lids should have a hole in the top, approximately the size of a nickel.

- Children transfer the beans from the cup to the tub with tweezers.

Puff Pictures

- Provide kitchen tongs or meatball presses.

- Give each child an outline of a snowman, a lamb or a bunny.

- Children paint glue inside the outline provided.

- Children use tongs to transfer cotton balls to the picture, dropping cotton balls inside the glued outline.

111

Torn Paper Art

- During circle time, stimulate the children's imaginations with a variety of torn paper shapes.

- Let the children express what they see — remembering that there are no wrong answers. *It Looked Like Spilt Milk* by Charles Green Shaw is a good book to read to stimulate their imaginations.

- Let the children tear paper into their own designs and use crayons for any details needed. The torn paper designs may be glued to a background.

Stocking Snakes

- Using the leg portion cut from panty hose, children stuff the stocking with styrofoam chips until they have achieved the length desired.

- Tie the stocking with masking tape or string.

- Eyes, tongue or stripes can be added with marking pens. The end result is a nice wiggly snake to take home.

Paper Folding

- Provide children with paper to fold (fan style).

- One by twelve inch strips of green construction paper make great worms.

- Regular (nine by twelve inch) construction paper makes a great fan.

Making Blocks

- Provide the children with large paper grocery sacks and a stack of old newspapers.

- Have children crumple newspaper and stuff each grocery sack (stuff firmly).

- Fold tops of grocery sacks down, square off and tape.

- Children can use these "blocks" to make forts or other structures in the block center.

* If a structure tumbles down, no one gets hurt by these lightweight blocks.

Spirals

- Using a coffee can lid as a stencil, have children trace a circle on a piece of construction paper.

- Draw a dotted "cut line" to create the spiral for the children to cut.

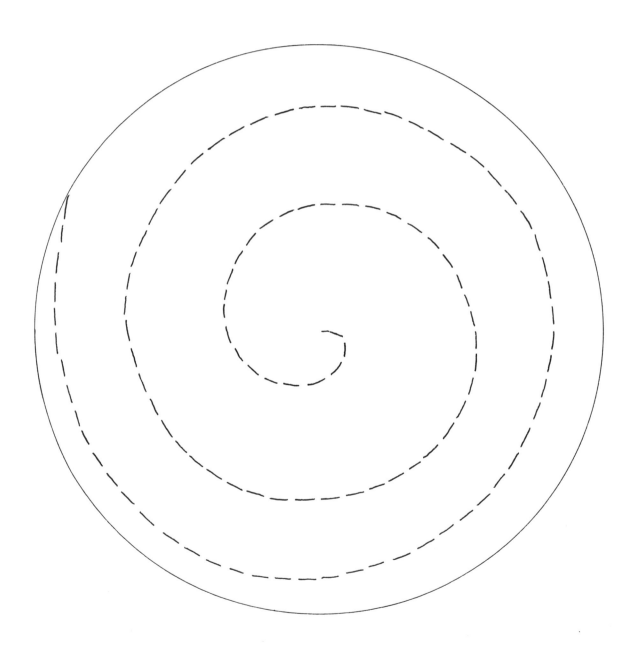

Holiday Straws

- Cut out shapes of hearts, shamrocks or Christmas trees.

- Cut two slits in the middle of the symbol.

- Put a straw through the slits to create a "Holiday Straw."

Rubbings

- Place a sheet of paper over cardboard bulletin board letters, leaves or paper dolls to create a rubbing.

- Children rub a crayon on paper until texture design underneath shows through.

- Items with different textures, such as sandpaper or nylon, also make good rubbings.

Bean Sweeping

- Provide the children with dried beans, a scoop and a small pastry brush.

- Have the children sweep the beans with the pastry brush into the scoop and transfer into a cup.

116

Animal Walk

- While singing to the melody of "Did You Ever See a Lassie," children take turns leading the group in moving like animals: "Did you ever see a rabbit, a rabbit, a rabbit? Did you ever see a rabbit go hopping like this?"

- Continue with bear-walking; snake-slithering; kangaroo-hopping; bird-flying; bug-crawling, etc.

117

Obstacle Course

- Arrange an obstacle course in the room that includes a tightrope to walk across (taped line), a table to crawl under, chairs to crawl around, a book to jump over and a box to crawl through.

- Following the leader, children walk, crawl and jump through the course.

✷ This is good for a rainy day.

Tire Hoops

- Gather old tires for the playground.

- Let children roll the tires across the playground.

- Limit use to a few small tires for safety.

Hula Hoop Toss

- Tape a hula hoop between two adult sized chairs or hang from the ceiling.

- Children take turns throwing bean bags, stocking balls or paper balls through the hoop.

Musical Cues

- Using recorded music, lead children in learning to skip and gallop around the room.

- Tape two records, such as "Skip to My Lou" and a cowboy song. Alternate the skipping and galloping music as you record them on the tape. When the tape is played, children will change from skipping to galloping, and vice versa, as the musical cues change.

Creepy Caterpillars

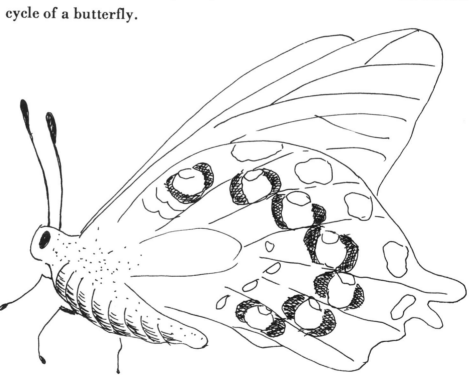

- Talk about caterpillars and look at several pictures of them.

- Have children lie on the floor and move the way caterpillars move, creeping and crawling.

- Children can pretend to make a cocoon and then come out of the cocoon and pretend to fly away as butterflies to demonstrate the life cycle of a butterfly.

Mirror Reflections

- Have children select a partner and stand facing each other.

- One child moves very slowly and the second child copies the movement.

- Use a variety of arm, leg and face movements.

Amazing Mazes

- Create a maze out of classroom items by moving tables and chairs and adding blocks and other classroom materials.

- Instruct children to go through the maze on their hands and knees, trying not to touch anything.

Trash Ball

- Using masking tape, place two tape lines on the floor, four to six feet apart.

- Children stand behind one line and toss crumpled balls of paper (trash balls) over the second line.

- Children count their successes and can tally them if desired.

Rainbows

- Use a large piece of mural paper taped to the wall.

- Provide a variety of colors of chalk or crayons.

- Play a record and let children make color sweeps back and forth in rainbow fashion on the drawing surface.

- Stop record periodically so children can change colors.

Junior Aerobics

- Use a record with a strong beat, such as a march.

- Let children take turns leading the group in appropriate exercises, such as lying on back and "riding a bicycle" with feet in air, jumping like jumping jacks, hugging alternate knees to chest or clawing at air with "tiger paws."

✱ Specific routines could be developed for added fun. This activity is a potential program for parents.

Bean Socks

- Cut off old socks at the ankles and partially fill with dried beans.

- Sew up the opening.

- Children can toss the beanbags to each other or at a target, such as a plastic tub or a circle taped on the floor.

Stocking Balls

- Cut toe off left leg of pantyhose.

- Begin rolling stocking from waists. Gather the right leg of the stocking into a ball and then roll into the left leg.

- Turn the cut toe of the left leg back over the rolled up ball and stitch the ends together.

- Give children a few of these safe balls to throw at a bucket, a taped circle or a plastic pool.

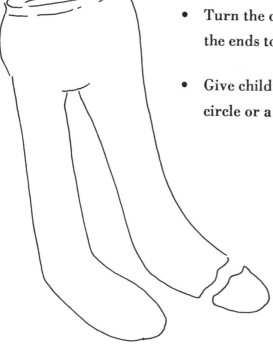

Blanket Toss

- In a variation of the Eskimo blanket toss, let several children hold the sides of a tablecloth or sheet, trying to move a ball on the sheet or tablecloth without dropping it on the floor.

- Music may be played while the children undulate the fabric.

Headbaskets

- Display pictures of individuals carrying heavy loads on their head.

- Provide baskets for children to try balancing on their heads.

- Safe objects, such as rolled up socks, could be placed nearby to load the baskets.

Hopscotch

- Draw a hopscotch pattern on the sidewalk or patio.

- Number the squares.

- Show children how to hop through the pattern.

- When one child has completed the pattern, another child takes a turn.

Statue of Liberty

- Cut butcher paper crowns; tape to fit each child's head.

- Provide newspaper, yellow tissue paper and masking tape. Children roll newspaper and tape; add a puff of tissue paper to the top of rolled newspaper to make a torch.

- Children then drape small sheets or white tablecloths around themselves.

- Put on a record and let children walk randomly around the room. When the music stops, children "freeze" like statues. Continue the music and freezes as long as desired.

Expanding Understanding

DEVELOPING LANGUAGE ARTS SKILLS

L anguage arts program for young children is rich with activities and experiences that encourage listening, speaking, writing and reading readiness. That young children are very sensitive to language is evident in the rapid development of language during the short period of the early childhood years. From the simple sentence structure used by a toddler, a progression is made to the more complex use of language by a five year old. "Me do" becomes "I will do it myself" in a brief time span.

Activities that stimulate listening and speaking encourage the complete development of oral language. Opportunities for children to increase vocabulary, develop concepts and use appropriate sentence structure are also necessary. Since children also learn from modeling, the teacher's use of language becomes a powerful teaching tool. The reading of books and telling of stories is critical to the development of language in its broadest sense. Children are not only building oral language but they are also beginning to understand the concept of written language.

Written language is developed through a long process. It is more than learning to use finger muscles to make letters, words and sentences. It is learning that writing is a way to communicate ideas to others. The concept of "talk written down" is developed as children become familiar with books and other types of print and as children see talk transcribed into writing. When a teacher labels an object, or writes down stories dictated by children, thereby demonstrating the use of written language, children will develop an interest in reading. Many children will begin writing on their own as soon as they are capable of making letters. It is not unusual for children to string a series of letters together and read it to a listener as if it really said something. This is called inventive spelling and will be referred to several times in this chapter.

The critical factor in the development of reading is opportunity for practice. Children must practice the many skills (mechanics) necessary for reading until they are "second nature" (internalized) and no longer require conscious thought. If children's thinking is cluttered with mechanics like which direction to move the eyes, which letter makes which sound, what the punctuation means and what a space means, they can't concentrate on meaning. Many early readers are not good readers because they have not internalized the skills necessary to move through written text without having to concentrate so hard on the mechanics. Children should never be pushed or rushed into reading. Children will read when they are ready — when all the "pieces" are in place. It is the teacher's role to provide opportunities to practice the necessary skills and develop the appropriate concepts.

Language arts in the early childhood classroom is integrated like all other curriculum areas. Good language lessons will arise and may be taught as part of math, science, social studies or any other area of the curriculum. Skills are best taught in a meaningful context, never in isolation. Language is a natural part of math, science and all curriculum areas just as it is a natural part of all life experiences each day. The goal of language is communication, and communication is essential to the well-being of mankind.

This chapter provides activities that develop the major language skills and concepts that are listed on the following page.

Auditory discrimination: the ability to recognize and identify sounds, to hear likenesses and differences.

Auditory memory: the ability to remember sounds after they have been heard.

Oral language: the ability to use language for self-expression.

Vocabulary development: the discovery of the meaning of words and the identification of new words.

Classification: the ability to categorize items or objects by like or common criteria.

Visual discrimination: the ability to see likenesses and differences.

Visual memory: the ability to remember what is seen and to identify items missing from what has been seen.

Left to right progression: the natural eye sweep needed for reading.

Hand-eye coordination: synchronizing the movement of the hand and the eyes.

Whole/part relationships: the ability to understand that parts make up a whole, for example, several letters make a word, or several pieces make a complete puzzle.

Written communication: the understanding that symbols communicate thoughts and feelings.

Comprehension: the understanding of concepts expressed through language.

133

Pick-a-Pair

- Make a tape of several sounds — some difficult and some less difficult. Example: door bell, telephone ring, fire engine, dog barking, baby crying, laughter, etc.

- Cut pictures from magazines to represent each sound.

- Have children listen to the tape and arrange the pictures in the same order as the sounds were heard on the tape.

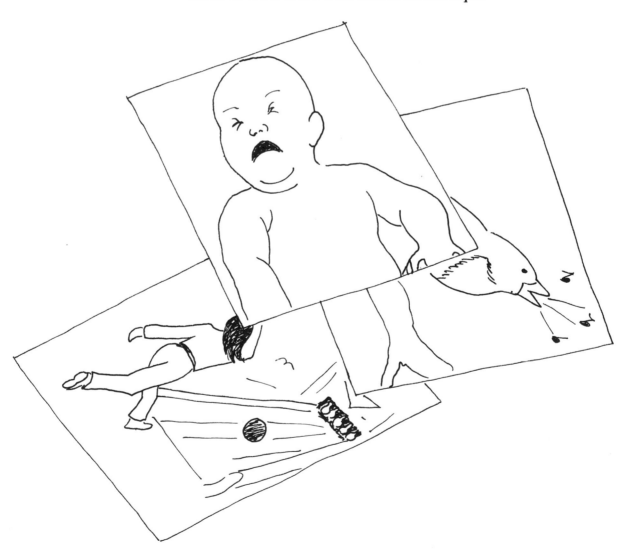

I've Got Rhythm

- Let each child create a rhythmic clapping pattern, for example, clap, snap; clap, snap; clap, snap — or clap, rest, rest; clap, rest, rest.

- Using a tape recorder, record each child's clapping pattern and let the children identify their own clapping pattern.

- Re-play tape and let children identify their classmates' clapping patterns.

Rhyming Time

- Prepare the children by reading stories and poems with rhyming words.

- Provide the children with a box of small toy objects.

- Ask the children to name each object.

- When the teacher is certain the children can correctly identify each object, the children can be asked to find objects with names that sound alike, for example, cake, rake; boy, toy, etc.

Match Makers

- Provide the children with three or four cans with lids, for example, potato chip cans or coffee cans, and a box of objects that can fit into the can.

- Allow the children to put objects in the cans. Then they shake the cans to determine which cans make the loudest sound, which cans make the softest sound.

✱ Cans can be ordered from softest to loudest.

Alliteration

- Give the children several examples of sentences with alliteration, such as Harry Hippo hops high, or Barney Bear bounces balls.

- Allow children to create their own sentences with words beginning with the same sound.

Name Game

- At opportune times during the day when it's necessary to call a child's name, use a teachable moment for children to learn rhyming sounds.

- Say, "Would the child whose name rhymes with TOY get in line."

- Roy or Joy or any other person with a name that rhymes responds to the request.

Do You Hear What I Hear?

- Group children in a circle.

- Place three rhythm band instruments in the center of the circle.

- While classmates have their eyes closed, one child sounds the instruments in an order of her choice.

- Another child is selected to repeat the order of sounds.

- To increase the level of difficulty, increase the number of instruments.

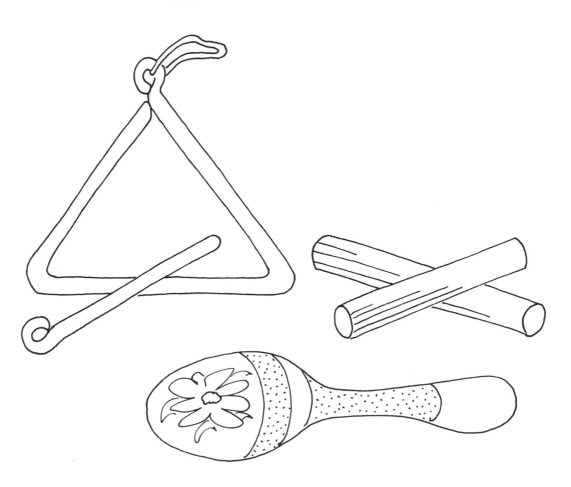

Silly Sentences

- Create a series of silly sentences for children to repeat.

  Examples: I know a lady with knobby knees.
  Who's always eating cheddar cheese.

  I like ice cream in my soup.
  By myself, or in a group.

Ears Up

- One child is selected as the leader.

- The leader gives directions to the group but the group follows only those directions preceded by the words "ears up," for example, "Ears up, touch your toes."

✱ This activity can be altered by inserting a new signal word, such as "blinking eyes," "snapping fingers," etc.

Go-fers

- The teacher selects a child to be the "Go-fer" and gives the "Go-fer" directions that contain two requests, for example, "Take the book to the table and pick up the scissors."

- If the child can handle two part directions, proceed to three, for example, "Take the cup to the shelf, close the drawer and bring a spoon to Jeff."

- Increase the difficulty of the directions as long as the child is able to comply.

Taped Directions for Art

- Prepare bubble liquid using one cup of water, three tablespoons of detergent and six tablespoons of tempera paint. Use different shaped containers for variations.

- Record the following directions on a tape recorder:

    1. Put the straw *in* the colored liquid you wish to use.

    2. Blow *into* the straw until bubbles stand *above* the *top* of the container.

    3. Place your paper *on top of* the bubbles.

    4. Press *down*.

    5. Turn your paper *over* and take a look.

- The children follow the taped directions to create a design on a sheet of paper.

★ This activity is great for teaching prepositions and concepts of position.

Rhyme Time

- Provide standard nursery rhyme books.

- When reading nursery rhymes stop at the ending rhyming word and let the children supply it. Example: "Jack be nimble, Jack be quick, Jack jumped over the _____."

Magic Mirror

- Have children sit in a circle.

- Pass around a hand mirror.

- Let each child make a statement about what he sees in the mirror.

- Let children draw pictures of themselves.

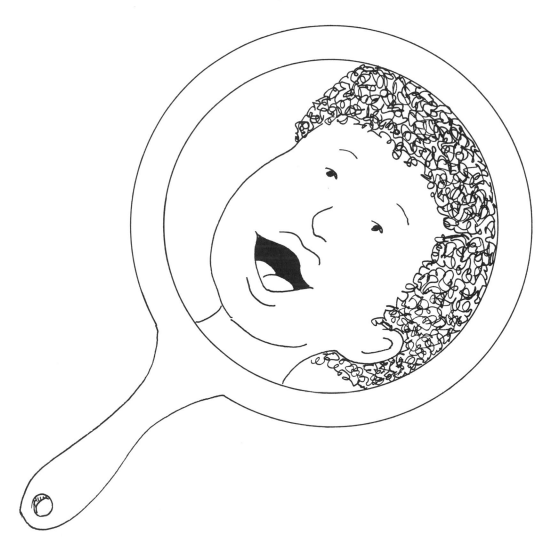

Magic Pebble

- Show children a pebble. Tell them you are pretending the pebble is magic and can grant wishes.

- Let each child hold the pebble and make a wish.

- Encourage the children to use complete sentences.

Pictures, Pictures, Pictures

- Develop a file of pictures from magazines.

- Children take turns describing how items are used, for example, chairs are for sitting, trees are for climbing, cars are for driving, etc.

Ticklers

- Have children lie on the floor on their backs with each child placing her head on another child's stomach.

- Tell the children to laugh.

- Let each child describe how it felt when everyone was laughing.

Sally Sad and Harriet Happy

- Prepare two paper plate faces on a stick, one with a happy face and one with a sad face.

- Let children take turns holding plate faces and explaining reasons for Sally being sad and Harriet being happy.

- Examples:

  "I'm Sally Sad, and I'm sad because…"
  "I'm Harriet Happy, and I'm happy because…"

In the Boat

- Using masking tape, tape a boat shape on the floor.

- Let children take turns standing in the "boat" and describing what they would do if they were in a real boat.

∗ Adaptation would be a taped rectangle to serve as a stage, with children describing what they would do on the stage.

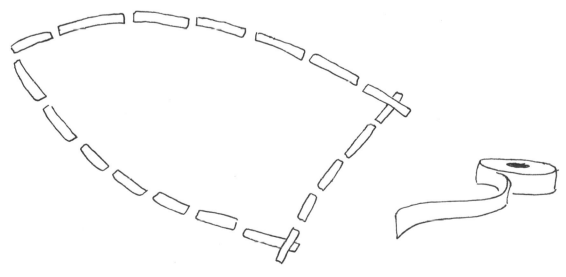

145

Deluxe
Show 'n Tell

- Have children bring an object from parents' workplace or from home. Tell them to talk to their parents about the use of the object.

- At circle time children take turns demonstrating and describing the item and its use. Example: "My daddy is a doctor, and he uses this stethoscope to listen to people's hearts." "My mother is a waitress, and she uses this pad to take orders."

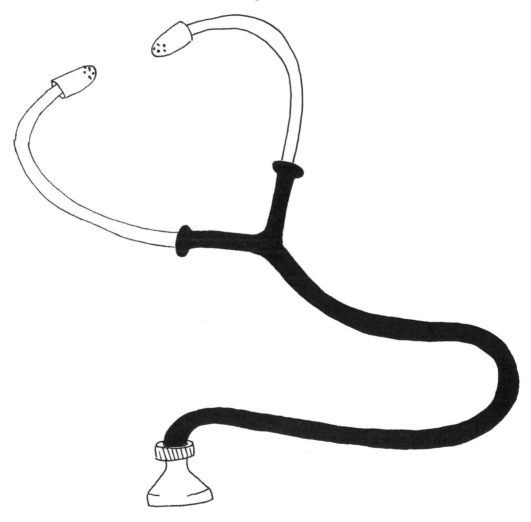

Puppet Party

- Provide children with paper plates, paper, crayons, glue and tongue depressors.

- Children draw faces on the plates and decorate the faces to create a puppet face. Tongue depressors are glued on the plates for handles.

- Children in pairs present a puppet show for the group.

- Be aware that young children are not capable of creating a plot, any dialogue created is acceptable.

I Spy

- The teacher selects a student to be "it" and that child starts the game by saying "I spy someone who is wearing red shoes and green pants."

- The rest of the children attempt to guess who is being described. If there is not enough information, the child who is "it" gives another clue.

- The first one to guess the correct person becomes the next "it."

Four Feelings

- Tell the following story:

  Joe got a brand new puppy for his birthday.

  He loved the puppy very much, but the puppy was very naughty.

  The first day he chewed up Daddy's slipper.

  The second day he chewed up the garbage sack and spilled garbage all over the kitchen floor.

  The third day he woke up everyone barking at the cat on the window sill.

  That day mother said, "No more puppy in the house."

- Ask the children questions about how Joe might have felt, how daddy might have felt, how mother might have felt and how the puppy might have felt.

String a Story

- While holding a ball of yarn in your hands, give the children a story starter. Example: "Yesterday I saw a green monster at the grocery store. He was..."

- Hold the end of the yarn and pass the ball to a child who will then add a made-up line to the story. When that child is finished, the ball of yarn is passed to another child.

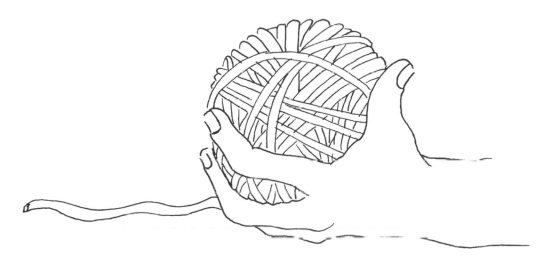

Guest Spot

- Bring to class an interesting object that will stimulate descriptions, statements and questions, such as a butterfly in a box, a stuffed animal, a goldfish or gerbil in a bowl.

- Encourage children to talk about the object. Ask open ended questions that require more than a yes or no response. Extend the childrens statements. Example: If the child says, "The fish is swimming," the teacher might add, "up and down in the bowl."

Let's Go Shopping

- During group time put several grocery store items in the middle of the circle. Hand a basket to one of the children and have the child find the item named in the following rhyme:

  (*child's name*) goes around, around
  Until he finds an (*grocery item*)
  (*child's name*) goes around, around

- Select another child and repeat the activity until all items are gone.

In the Bag

- Put several items into a purse, briefcase or bag.

- Children describe the items they find in the purse, briefcase or bag.

- After the children are experienced, one child can describe the item without letting the other children see it and the other children try to guess what the item is.

✱ This activity offers a good opportunity for the teacher to expand the vocabulary of the children by asking questions about each item.

Positional Words

- Give each child, or a few children, a beanbag.

- Ask children to put beanbag *on* their shoulder, *under* their chin, *beside* their shoe, *on top* of their head, etc.

What Is It?

- After reading a story, choose a word or two to extend through discussion.

- Example: "In the story, Jerry sat on a *stump*. What is a stump? Do we have one in our room? Where might we find a stump?"

People and Animals

- Cut out eight to ten magazine pictures of people; cut out an equal number of animals.

- Paste pictures on cards, reserving one picture from each category.

- Paste the extra pictures on the outside of each of two manila folders.

- Children take the cards and classify them, putting all the people in the people folder and all the animals in the animal folder.

Land and Water

- Cut a posterboard in half. Glue the halves back together with masking tape to make a hinge.

- Open the poster folder. On one side draw waves. On the other side draw a landscape.

- Provide children with a variety of pictures of things that live on land (squirrels, dogs, people) and things that live in the sea (whale, star fish, crabs).

- Children place the pictures on the correct side of the poster folder.

* Pictures can be stored in the closed posterboard folder.

Sorting Socks

- Collect a number of pairs of old socks.

- Keep in a box for children's use.

- Children match the socks and fold the tops over to make a pair.

Pantry Game

- Collect a duplicate set of labels from canned goods and food boxes — tuna fish, vegetable soup, shredded wheat, rice, etc.

- Paste one set of labels on a posterboard.

- Children match the second set to the ones on the posterboard.

Opposites

- Gather several items that are opposites, for example, a big block, a little block; a tall glass, a short glass; a clean glass, a dirty glass, etc.

- Have children pair the items that are opposites.

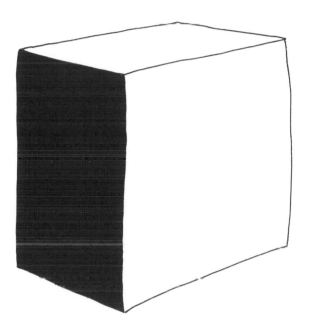

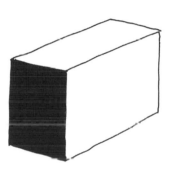

Face to Face

- Cut ten circles from durable paper, for example, tagboard, wallpaper, posterboard, etc.

- Draw five sets of matching faces on the circles.

- Children find matching pairs of faces.

- To increase the difficulty, increase the number of face pairs and decrease the level of distinct features.

Wallpaper Lotto

- Cut eighteen different patterns of wallpaper into duplicate two inch squares.

- Cut two six inch squares of cardboard and section off into nine two inch squares to create lotto boards. Glue nine two inch wallpaper squares on the lotto boards. Reserve the duplicate squares for playing cards.

- Two children may play the game. Provide each child with one of the lotto boards. Turn the lotto playing cards face down. Each child takes a turn drawing a card and attempting to match the squares on her lotto board. Matches are placed on the board, non-matches are turned face down and used when the first stack of cards runs out. Game ends when both children cover their lotto boards completely.

Greeting Cards

- Collect old Christmas greeting cards.

- Cut cards into halves, thirds or fourths, depending on the developmental level of the class.

- Have the children match the cards and paste them back together on a construction paper background.

Holiday Adaptations: Present this activity at Christmas, using Christmas cards; on Valentine's Day, using valentines; at Easter, using Easter cards, etc.

Toppers

- Collect a number of food containers with plastic lids, for example, potato chip cans, butter tubs, microwave dinner dishes, etc.

- Place lids and containers on a table and let children place matching lids on correct containers.

Roll Call

- Prepare a name card for each child in the class.

- Use the name cards to direct children for transitional activities or for playing games.

  Examples: "This little boy (teacher shows name) may go to the snack table."

  "This little girl can take a bow."

Freckle Names

- Write each child's name on construction paper.

- Have children outline their names with glue on construction paper.

- Give each child a handful of hole punches from the collage box and have them sprinkle these over the paper. Shake off the excess onto a newspaper.

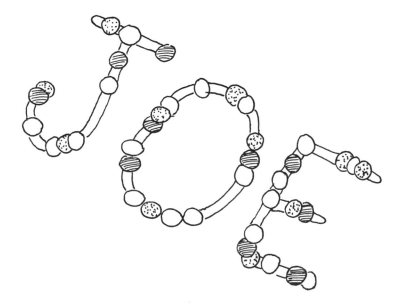

Bean Plates

- Prepare a "table tent" for each child by folding a long piece of cardboard in half.

- Print each child's name on a tent.

- Have children outline names with Q-tip and glue.

- Sprinkle beans over letter oulined with glue. Shake off excess.

- Use as name plates for seating at lunch.

Mail for the Letter Carrier

- Print each child's name on an envelope.

- Give each child a matching name card to hold up.

- With children sitting in a circle, have children take turns delivering the mail — matching envelope to name card.

- Surprise gifts could be placed in envelopes, such as a pressed flower, a sticker, a picture, etc.

Sand Letters

- Provide children with cards that have a large alphabet letter drawn on them.

- Give children a Q-tip to apply glue to the outline of the letter.

- Have children sprinkle sand over the glue and shake off excess. A three-dimensional letter is created to use and re-use for letter recognition.

Slinky Letters

- Provide a large line drawing of an alphabet letter for each child.

- Children dip a length of yarn into a bowl of liquid starch.

- The yarn is placed on the letter configuration.

- When dry, a tactile letter has been formed.

On Stage

- Draw large letters on each of 26 squares of cardboard. Attach each letter to a string to make a necklace. Give one card necklace to each child. (If the class is small, teacher can substitute by taking excess letters.)

- Teacher announces each alphabet letter with "Ladies and Gentlemen, may I present 'Mister A'," etc.

- As each letter is announced, the child goes to the front of the room and performs an activity of his choice, such as jumping up and down, twirling around, bowing, etc.

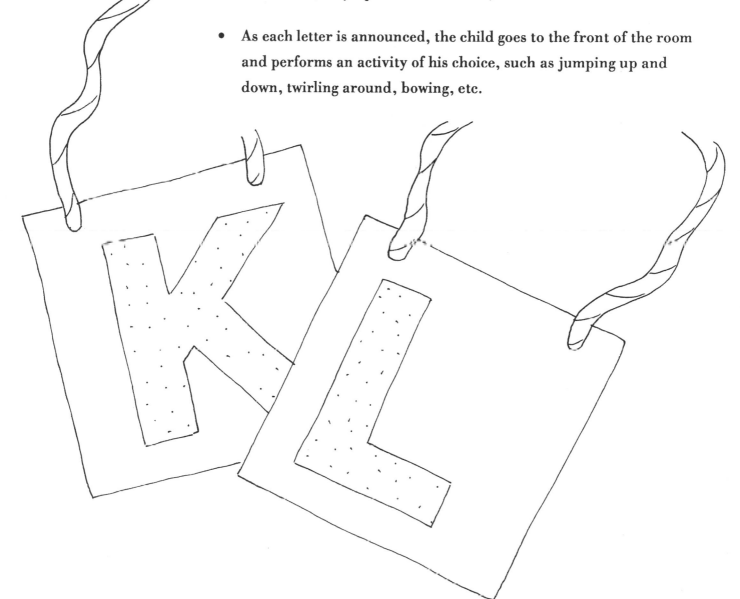

161

Lacing Letter

- Make a twelve inch cardboard set of several letters. Punch holes in the outline of each letter about one inch apart. Attach a two foot piece of yarn to the letter.

- Allow children to lace the outline of the letter.

Playdough Letters

- Using your favorite playdough recipe, let children form large alphabet letters.

- An alternate method could be making the letters on top of an alphabet card.

✱ (See pages 46 and 47 for two playdough recipes.)

Pretzel Letters

- Prepare pretzel dough:

  1 1/2 cups warm water   1 envelope of yeast

  4 cups flour   1 tsp. salt

  Mix all ingredients.

- Give each of the children enough dough to shape into the first letter of their name.

- Brush dough letters with beaten egg and sprinkle with coarse salt.

- Bake at 425 degrees for twelve minutes.

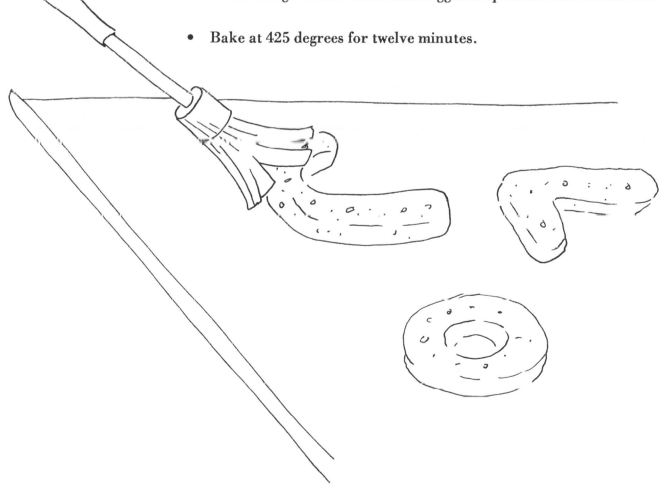

Tablecloth Lotto

- Tape butcher paper to a table and print the alphabet on it.

- Make a set of matching alphabet index cards.

- Have children match the cards to the letters on the tablecloth.

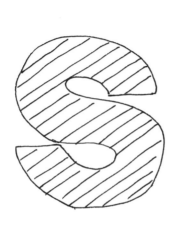

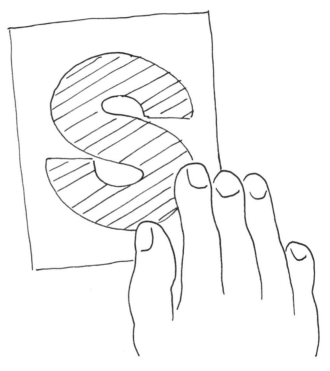

Heart to Heart

- Cut 52 construction paper hearts.

- Write duplicate upper case letters to create 26 pairs of hearts.

- Children match hearts by matching letters.

- Difficulty can be increased by making upper and lower case letter pairs to match.

Lucky Letters

- Write alphabet letters on each of 26 large cards. Make a matching set of small cards.

- Place large cards on the floor in a circle in alphabetical order.

- Put on a record and have children walk around the circle of cards.

- When the music stops, children pick up the letter card closest to them.

- Teacher holds up the small card with an alphabet letter.

    Example: *H* — Child holding H comes into the middle of the circle and sits.

165

Bingo

- Prepare bingo gameboards labeled with letters. Provide beans or buttons for markers.

- Teacher randomly draws letters from a bowl. Showing letter drawn, teacher announces letter to be covered on bingo card.

- Children cover the letter if it is on their card.

- Game ends when one child covers all her letters on her bingo card.

What's Missing?

- Provide children with a box of small objects, for example, crayon, scissors, pencil, paste jar, book, etc.

- Let the children select four items.

- Have the children close their eyes, then remove one of the items.

- Ask the children to tell you what's missing.

- Continue the game, changing the items.

What's the Order?

- Collect three or four items from around the classroom, for example, block, crayon, book, doll, etc.

- Arrange the items in a specific order.

- Ask the children to close their eyes.

- Change the order of the items.

- Ask one child to put the items back in the original order.

* This activity may be done with objects specific to an area of study.

* Flannel board items may also be used.

Can You Remember?

- With children in a circle, have them close their eyes and ask them questions such as:

  "What color is the bathroom door?"

  "What did we tape on the window yesterday?"

Holiday Adaptations: "What are the names of the things we have on the Christmas tree?" (ornaments, popcorn string, icicles, etc.) "How many bunnies are on the bulletin board?"

Whoops!

- Draw a number of large objects or people on a chart. Leave off a major feature, for example, a leg from a table, an eyebrow from a face, a wheel from a car, etc.

- Have children describe what is missing.

- As children become more proficient, increase the complexity of the missing item (a button from a shirt, a lace from a shoe, etc.)

Cozy Comics

- Cut out comic strips from the Sunday paper and bring them to class.

- During times when the teacher can work with children individually or in small groups, read the comics to children.

- Point to pictures in left to right order as the comics are read.

Marking Time

- Provide each child with a ruled construction paper attendance chart.

- Child marks the squares in left to right order for each day of attendance.

* This process helps children internalize left to right progression.

170

Back Together Again

- Cut large magazine pictures into three or four vertical strips.

- Let children glue pictures back together on a background of construction paper.

Broken Names

- Write each child's name on a large card.

- Cut the card into puzzle pieces, making each letter a puzzle piece.

- Children put letters back together to spell their names correctly.

- Make the name cards self-correcting by making each cut between letters different.

171

Labels

- Label objects and areas in the room, for example, Book Center, Piano, Cubby Holes, etc.

* Labeling helps develop the concept that written symbols represent the spoken word.

Name Tags

- As each child comes in the room, teacher asks their name and writes it on a self-adhesive name tag (the kind parents wear to conferences).

- Children observe their spoken name transcribed to a written name.

- Children wear the name tags all day, and observe the other written names.

* On another day, the same activity may be used with first and last names.

Funny Funny Papers

- Provide each child with a comic strip with the words in the strip blanked out. (White-out works well.)

- Let the children create their own version of the story by telling the story they see in the pictures.

- Dictated stories can be written by the teacher in the blanked out spaces so that children develop the concept that writing is talk written down.

173

Writing Rhymes

- Read several simple rhymes for children. Nursery rhymes provide a good examples of simple rhymes.

- Make up a rhyme with the children and write it on a flip chart.

  Examples: Jogging is fun.
  If you like to run.

  Walking is great.
  But don't be late.

Lists

- Find opportunities for children to see the teacher writing names. This helps the children understand the relationship between the spoken name and written name.

- Make charts for the class roll; make helpers' charts and make lists of children who have had turns on a toy.

My Journal

- Take several sheets of white paper and one piece of colored construction paper, fold in half and staple with the colored paper on the outside.

- Each day have children write or draw on a page of this journal. They can draw a picture for the day or use "make believe" letters to write down their thoughts for the day.

- Provide an opportunity for children to "read" a journal page to someone else.

- What they write is not important. It's the concept that should be stressed.

✳ This activity helps children understand that their thoughts can be communicated through symbols.

Experience Charts

- Write experiences or feelings about experiences on a chart as children describe them orally:

> We went to the barn.
>
> We saw cows and horses
>
> We played in the hay.
>
> The hay smelled good.

✶ This is one of multiple opportunities for children to describe events and see them transcribed into written form.

Rebus Charts

- Write the experiences of the children on charts and add drawings beside or over certain NOUNS:

I went to the rodeo and wore my hat (drawing) and my new boots (drawing).

- Let children help you "re-read" what was written.

Baggie Book

- Staple six baggies together at the bottom of the bags and put a strip of masking tape or colored tape over the staples to form the spine of the book.

- Cut pieces of tagboard or construction paper an appropriate size for fitting into each baggie.

- Let children dictate and illustrate a story to go on the pages and then place them in proper sequence inside the baggies.

- Stories can be changed easily by removing current pages and replacing with a new story.

- Popular stories can be used as models for children to imitate, for example, *Brown Bear, Brown Bear* by Bill Martin, Jr. may become Black Cat, Black Cat.

Pen Pals

- Keep a supply of envelopes readily available for children.

- Encourage children to draw pictures that tell their friend something or to use inventive spelling to convey a message. Children can also use the teacher as a scribe.

- When letters are complete, have children put them in envelopes and deliver them to their friends' cubby holes.

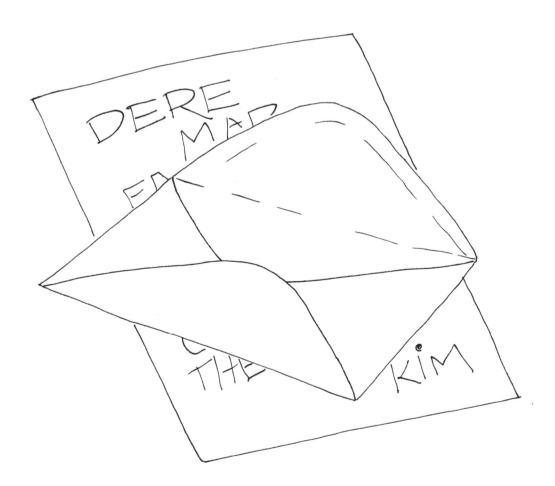

Nature Bracelet

- Wrap a piece of masking tape (sticky side out) around each child's wrist.

- Give each child a printed list of pictures with labels, such as a flower, grass, a seed, a leaf. Review the list orally with class.

- Children go outside with the list and find the objects. As they find each object, they place it on their nature bracelet. Review the list and findings with the class when all are finished.

Go-Togethers

- Gather a group of items that includes pairs of items that go together:

        shoe — sock

        pencil — paper

        comb — brush

        soap — wash cloth

        flower — vase

- Mix up the items.

- Let children take turns matching items that go together.

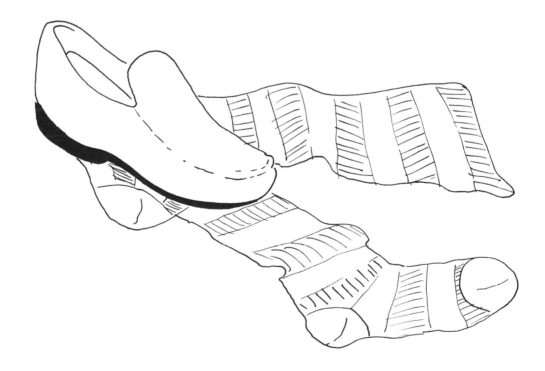

True/Not True

- Present children with pairs of sentences — one that is true and one that is untrue.

    Example: Everyone in this classroom is a boy./This class is made up of ____girls and ____boys.

- Let children select the true statement.

- After children are confident in selecting this type of categorical statement, present sentence pairs in which one sentence is partially true and the other sentence is completely true.

Story Detectives

- After reading a story to children, give multiple choices to questions.

    Example: After the story of *Little Red Riding Hood*, ask children to select the right answer to this question: What was Little Red Riding Hood carrying to her grandmother's house? (a briefcase, a purse, a basket or a box)

✱ One or two questions of this type after a story help children become familiar with this type of questioning strategy.

First Things First

MAKING
MATH MEANINGFUL

ath for young children must be concrete and filled with play and exploration. It is important that young children truly understand foundation concepts before moving on to more abstract operations like addition and subtraction. There is a developmental sequence for teaching math. If teachers adhere to this sequence and provide children with a multitude of opportunities for practicing and internalizing math, young children will be prepared for higher level activities when they are introduced. Rote counting to 30 does not mean that a child understands the concept of 30. If you let children count 30 marbles into a tall slender glass and 30 marbles into a small shallow bowl and then ask them which container has more marbles, they will very happily tell you that there are more marbles in the tall slender glass. So take time to develop concepts thoroughly. Don't rush. Children will learn to count as counting becomes meaningful to them.

The following is a list of math concepts and definitions for young children. The list is developmentally sequenced meaning that the list begins with the first math skill the child needs to internalize and each consecutive skill is built on the understanding of the preceding skill.

Classification — The process of grouping or sorting objects into classes or categories according to a systematic characteristic, criteria or principle.

Patterning — The process of creating repetitions of symbols or objects.

One-to-one correspondence — The process of pairing or matching items or objects, for example, one napkin for each person.

185

Ordering and sequencing — The process of ordering relationships, for example, smallest to largest or lightest to heaviest or least to most.

Numeration — The ability to recognize numerals and place a correct numeral with a given number of objects. Three is a number, 3 is a numeral.

Measurement — The comparison of items by a standard unit.

Addition — The joining of sets.

Subtraction — The separation of sets.

Graphing — The process of classifying data.

Fractions — A method of dividing items fairly.

Using "teachable moments" is very valuable in teaching math, for example, count boys in the line and then girls in the line, count number of jumping jacks during exercise and number of cookies during snack. This is using math and counting in the meaningful context of everyday experiences.

This and That

- Place a strip of masking tape on the floor.

- Have a boy stand on one side of the tape line and a girl on the other.

- Ask the class what is different about the two people.

- When someone identifies the distinguishing characteristic as being boy/girl, bring another child up and ask where he or she should go.

- Give each child a turn.

✳ Continue this activity from time to time using other classification criteria, such as type of shoes worn, color of clothing, age, etc. Classification can also be reinforced with everyday activities (all the children with white shoes may go to the snack table).

Classification Books

- Use two pieces of construction paper to make a book.

- With the children, look through old magazines and newspapers for pictures of people and animals.

- Have the children cut out the pictures and paste them on the people page or the animal page.

Button to Button

- Collect several different types of buttons, for example, one hole, two hole, four hole, red, white, black, blue, round, square, etc.

- Take an egg carton and glue one button on the inside of each section of the egg carton.

- Allow children to sort the remaining buttons into the sections according to an established criteria, such as number of holes, color, shape, etc.

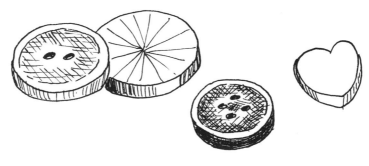

Shoes, Shoes, Shoes

- Have children take off their shoes.

- Classify shoes according to types — tennis shoes, dress shoes, oxfords — or according to how the shoes fasten —buckle shoes, tie shoes, slip-ons or velcro clasp shoes.

Shape Match

- Prepare a shape chart. Cut out a variety of colorful circles, triangles and squares.

- Have the children paste the shapes in the corresponding column, thus making a column of circles, a column of triangles and a column of squares.

- Progress to more difficult shapes as the children are ready.

Holiday Adaptations: Use the same chart format, but create new categories, such as pumpkins with different facial expressions for Halloween, different shaped leaves for fall, different colored ornaments for Christmas and different size hearts for Valentine's Day.

Thing That Are; Things That Are Not

- Put several items in a Ziploc bag, such as a pipe cleaner, a paper clip, a crayon, a dried bean, a penny and a clothespin.

- Allow children to classify the items in the bag according to their own established criteria, but using the language "Things that are; things that are not."

- For example a child might place the pipe cleaner, paper clip and clothespin into one pile, and the remaining items into another pile and say, "Things that are fasteners and things that are not fasteners."

* This type of classifying allows children to see multiple attributes of an item and also increases the child's awareness of how to develop classifying criteria.

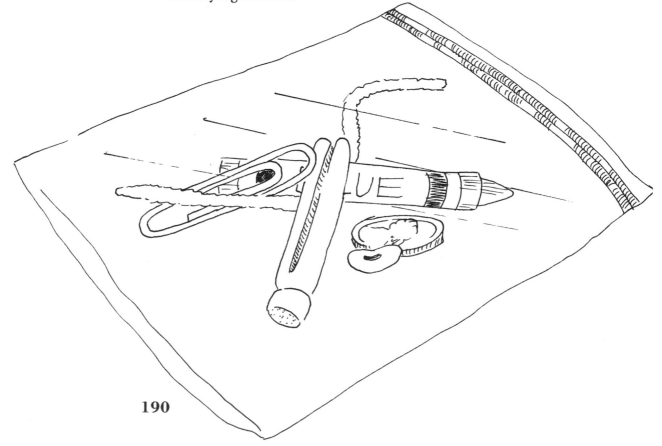

Shape Hunt

- Cut out two circles, two squares, two triangles and two rectangles.

- Hide one set of shapes somewhere in the room (each shape in a different place).

- Have the children take turns. Give a child one shape at a time and have him try to find the matching shape until all four are found.

Musical Shapes

- Cut out several squares, circles, triangles and rectangles from posterboard.

- Place the shapes on the floor in a circle.

- Play a favorite record and have children walk around the circle until the music stops.

- When the music stops, children should put their toe on the shape closest to them.

- Ask each child to name the shape her toe is touching.

People Patterns

- Seat six children in a line alternating the direction they are facing.

- When the class has identified the pattern as facing front, facing back, have each child in turn continue the pattern by sitting in the correct direction.

- Verbalize the pattern as children are placed, front/back, front/back.

✳ At another time assist the children in creating other people patterns, such as stand/sit, arms up/arms down, etc.

Object Patterns

- Place common objects such as plastic forks, jar lids or cups on a table.

- Create a pattern by placing objects into a repetitive sequence, for example, cup/jar lid/fork, cup/jar lid/fork.

- Allow children to first copy the established pattern, then create their own.

Paper Patterns

- Cut circles, squares and triangles that are all the same color.

- Allow children to create patterns with the geometric shapes on adding machine tape or other horizontal strips of paper.

- After exploring various patterning possibilities, the children may glue their favorite pattern on the paper.

Holiday Adaptations: Provide children with holiday patterns, such as pumpkins, ghosts and witches for Halloween or trees, stars and balls for Christmas. Follow the paper patterning process described above.

Crayon Patterns

- Empty several boxes of crayons onto the table or floor.

- Allow children to create a pattern with the crayons — two red crayons, one purple crayon, two red crayons.

Paper Chain

- Cut sheets of colored paper into one by nine inch strips. Use at least two colors but not more than three colors.

- Have children glue strips of paper to form a color patterned chain.

- Use chains as necklaces, bracelets or room decorations.

Set Patterns

- Provide the children with a handful of dried beans or any other easy to handle small counter.

- Have children work with the teacher creating patterns of one bean/two beans, one bean/two beans, etc.

- Allow children to create their own patterns of number sets.

Teacher's Helper

- Allow children to take turns passing out napkins, cups, books, cookies, etc. to their classmates.

- This kind of activity will prove a first hand experience with matching one-to-one. Young children will keep passing the items until they are all gone, instead of realizing they should stop when everyone has one. Practice develops understanding.

One Pebble for Every Child

- Bring a sack of pebbles or marbles to the circle. Give each child a pebble.

- Tell the children that we are going to see if all the children who are in the circle now will be in the circle after bathroom break, center time or outdoor play, whichever fits the schedule.

- Have the children put their pebble back in the sack when they leave the circle.

- When the circle reconvenes, hand each child a pebble and then show the children that the sack is empty.

- Repeat the phrase, one child for every pebble, several times throughout the activity.

✶ The language one *pebble* for every *child* and one *child* for every *pebble* is a good way to help children conceptualize one-to-one matching.

Flowers on Stems

• Let children make flowers from coffee filters or cupcake holders by dripping colored water from an eyedropper onto the filters or holders.

• Cut strips of green paper (approximately one inch wide) to create stems.

• Allow children to match one flower to one stem and glue on a mural or staple to a bulletin board.

Sails

• Cut simple boats from construction paper.

• Cut triangular sails from white construction paper.

• Allow children to match one sail to each boat and one boat to each sail.

✳ Do the same activity matching strings to kites, peanuts to elephants and bones to dogs.

Ice Cream Cones

- Prepare outlines of ice cream cones on sheets of construction paper. Cut out paper "scoops" of ice cream.

- Have the children paste a "scoop" of ice cream on each cone, thereby matching one to one.

✳ Make up other games, such as matching hats to heads, dogs to bones, etc.

Holiday Adaptations: Prepare outlines of flag poles for the Fourth of July or trees for Christmas. Have children paste flags on the poles for the Fourth of July or stars on top of trees for Christmas.

Pennies

- Take ten index cards and use a penny to trace circles on the index cards; one circle on the first card, two circles on the next, three on the next, etc.

- Allow children to match pennies to circles; one penny for each circle, one circle for each penny.

Egg Weigh

- Collect some eggs (for example, from pantyhose or plastic Easter eggs) and place inside them items, such as pebbles, spool of thread, paper clips, etc.

- Have children take turns placing the eggs in order from heavy to light.

- Extend this activity using more eggs or by having the children pair eggs that seem to weigh the same, and then, perhaps, seeing the items that are inside.

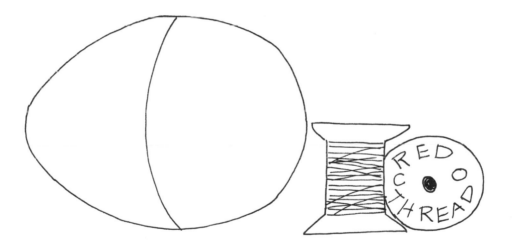

Long and Short Caterpillars

- Cut eggs cartons into different lengths to make caterpillars.

- Allow the children to decorate them with paper scraps (optional).

- Have the children arrange the caterpillars in order from longest to shortest.

Concentric Circles

- Cut circles of various sizes out of wallpaper scraps, construction paper, etc.

- The teacher should sort the circles according to size to aid the children in visual discrimination of different sizes.

- Allow the children to create concentric circles in designs of their own choosing by gluing smaller circles on top of larger ones.

- Use size comparative terms as you work with the children, for example, small, smaller, smallest; big, bigger, biggest.

Holiday Adaptations: Cut varying sizes of bats for Halloween, snowballs for Christmas or eggs for Easter. Guide children in ordering from smallest to largest or largest to smallest.

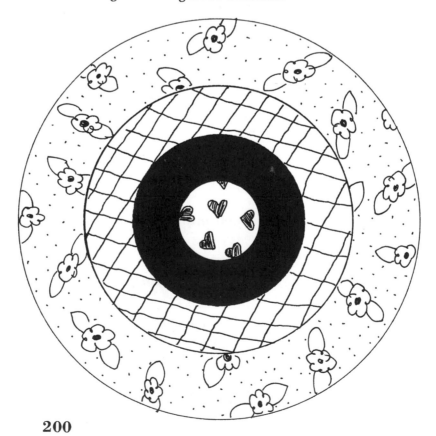

Christmas Tree Surprise

- Provide child with paper cupcake holders.

- Have children arrange cupcake holders in lines of one, two, three, four, etc., beginning with one at the top and moving down. The cupcake holder can be stapled to a bulletin board if desired.

- Let children identify the resulting shape.

Carlos the Caterpillar

- Have children trace large circles on green paper. (The inside of a roll of masking tape makes an easily traceable shape.) The teacher numbers the circles 1, 2, 3, 4, etc., so that the children can paste them in numerical order.

- The children then cut out circles and paste them together by overlapping slightly.

- Small strips of paper can be available for adding "feet."

Going Fishing

- Cut cardboard fish into different lengths (for example, three inches, four inches, five inches, six inches), and attach a paper clip to each fish.

- Make a fishing pole with a dowel and a magnet tied to the end of fishing line or a string. Your pond can be a box or just a piece of blue construction paper on the floor.

- Have children catch fish by touching the magnet to the paper clip, and as they catch the fish, have them arrange from smallest to largest.

* A variation might be for each child to catch only five fish. If a fish has the same length as one already caught, it is put back into the pond. When each child has caught five fish, see who has caught the longest line of fish by placing the fish tail to mouth.

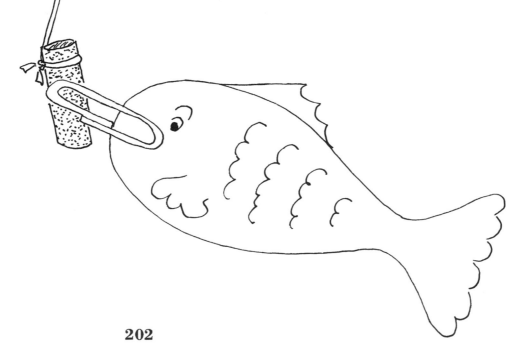

Fishing Line

- Prepare a fishing line with numbered clothespins (one through ten) on it. The clothespins should be in sequential order.

- Draw and cut out ten fish; write numerals one through ten on them.

- Have children place numbered fish on the line by matching the correct numerals.

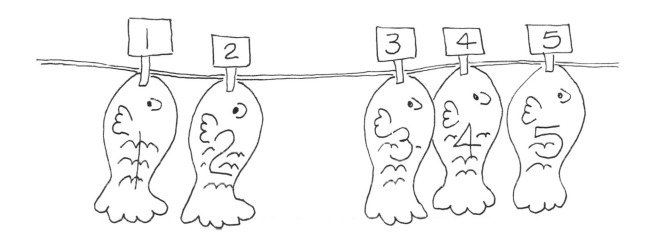

Number Bingo

- Make a "Bingo" card, approximately four by five inches, and divide it into one inch squares. Create a free space on the card and randomly number the other squares 0 - 10, using some numerals more than once.

- Hold up a large numeral, such as a 2. Let the children find all the 2's on their cards and cover them with a button, bottle cap, bean, cardboard square, etc.

Thumbprint Numerals

- Write large numerals on sheets of paper, then have children press their thumbs on an ink pad and trace over the configuration of the numerals with their thumbprints.

- After the thumb printing is complete, have children draw (or cut and paste) the appropriate number of objects on the paper.

* This is a good paper for sending home. Remember to write numeral recognition on the bottom of the paper for communication with parents.

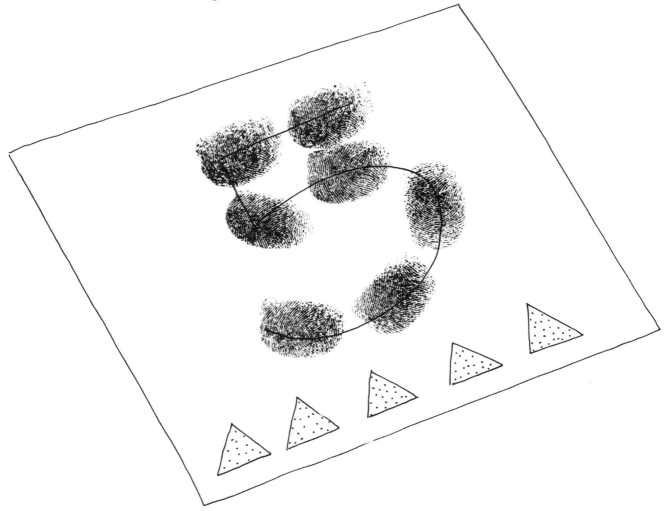

Egg Carton Toss

- Number the sections of an egg carton from one to ten, leaving a section on either end blank.

- Draw or paste a picture of a dog on one blank section and a cat on the other.

- Have children take turns tossing ping-pong balls into the carton. If the ball goes into the dog section, the player barks — if it goes into the cat section, the player meows. If the ball lands in a numbered section, the numeral is named.

205

Musical Numbers

- Prepare large and small cards with numerals on them.

- Place the large numeral cards on the floor in a circle and have children walk around the circle while a record plays.

- When the music stops, each child puts his toe on a numeral card. The teacher holds up a small numeral card, calling its name, and each child looks to see who is standing by the corresponding large numeral card. Example: "Jim has his toe on numeral 6," etc.

- Play resumes when the music starts again and the children once again walk around the circle.

Card Match (modified "Go Fishing")

- Provide children with a deck of regular playing cards, using only the number cards two through ten.

- Let children play "Go Fishing."

- Each child has a turn to ask other players for all their two's, three's, etc. The child must have at least one of the cards she is asking for in her own hand. The object is to get all four suits of each numeral.

Card Matching

- Use old decks of cards to create a matching game by taking one set of cards, two through ten, and gluing them down in a folder or a on a piece of posterboard.

- Use the remainder of the deck as matching cards.

- Children can match other cards, two through ten, to the set that has been glued down.

Calendar Match

- Cut up old calendars to create matching cards.

- Leave one page of the calendar intact to be the mat for matching the cut-up calendar pieces.

Number Clips

- Write numerals one to ten on ten index cards.

- Provide the children with paper clips and the numbered index cards and ask them to attach the number of clips on each card to correspond with the printed numeral.

My Number Book

- Fold two or three pieces of construction paper in half and staple to make a book.

- Print "My Number Book" on the cover.

- Write one numeral on each page of the book.

- Allow children to paste stickers, stamps or cut-out magazine pictures on each page to correspond with the numeral on that page.

Piggy Banks

- Punch slots in the lids of ten baby food jars.

- Write the numbers one through ten on the jars.

- Give the children some pennies and have them drop the appropriate number into each "piggy bank."

Questions
to ask:

How many pennies will you put into this bank?

Could you put the banks in order from one to ten?

Which bank has the most money in it? The least?

If you wanted to buy a piece of penny bubble gum, which bank would you get the money out of?

If I wanted you to give me six cents from two banks, which two would you use? How about eight cents?

Show me a bank that has the same number of pennies as your age.

Count all the pennies and tell me how many there are.

Pasting Sets

- Prepare a number chart as seen below. Cut out a variety of colorful circles or squares.

- Help children paste the correct number of circles by each numeral on the chart.

- Progress to higher numbers as the children are ready.

Christmas Tree Decorating

- Cut out trees from green construction paper and yellow stars from felt.

- Glue a star at the top of each tree and number them from one to five.

- Cut out fifteen small red balls or circles. Have the children place as many red balls on the trees as specified by the numeral on the stars.

Holiday Adaptation: This activity could also be used for other seasons — baskets and Easter eggs.

Mix It Myself Snack

- Provide children with numeral cards that indicate the number of items they should count into their snack cup. Easy items for the snack mix are miniature marshmallows, raisins, peanuts and sunflower seeds.

- To create their snack, children are instructed to count five raisins, eight marshmallows, seven sunflower seeds and four peanuts.

Beanbag Throw

- Set a wastebasket or box in an open space.

- Put down a masking tape line six to eight feet away from the container.

- Have the children stand behind the line and take turns throwing beanbags into the basket, allowing each child five to ten throws.

- Have the children count the number of beanbags in the basket to figure their scores.

Strawberry Container Zoo

- Cut construction paper into squares small enough to place on the bottom of strawberry containers.

- Draw a numeral from one to ten on the bottom of each container with a permanent marker.

- The strawberry containers serve as zoo cages when turned upside down. Have the children place the appropriate number of animals beneath each cage.

- The animals may be pictures cut from magazines or small plastic animals.

How Many Popsicle Sticks?

- Cover juice cans with solid contact paper and write a numeral from zero through ten on each.

- Glue the corresponding number of stars on each can.

- Place the cans and popsicle sticks on a table. Ask children to place the appropriate amount of popsicle sticks into each can, corresponding with the numeral or the number of stars.

Plates and Clips

- Write the numeral one through ten on ten paper plates.

- Hook paper clips together into sets.

- Have children match the paper clip chains to the numerals on plates.

✶ For a variation, create sets by putting reinforcement stickers on index cards or by punching holes in index cards.

Math Number Bags

- Spray large beans desired colors with enamel paint; allow drying time. Spray the back of the beans. (This step is optional, plain lima beans can be used.)

- When beans are completely dry, place the desired number of beans in a Ziploc bag and close it.

- With a marker, write the number of beans on the bottom of the bag. Draw a vertical line down the middle of the bag.

- Let children move the beans from one side to the other, leaving beans on either side of the bag. Help them to note that the total number of beans in the bag always remains the same. For example, if five beans are in the bag, children can manipulate the beans to see combinations that make five — two beans on one side of the vertical line and three beans on the other side.

Golf Tee Combinations

- Write the numbers one through five on various margarine tub lids.

- Place twice that number of golf tees in each tub (half one color and half a second color) as is indicated on the lid. For example, if the top of the container says five, place five white tees in the container and five red tees in the container.

- Punch the same number of holes in each lid as the number on the top. Then have the children make combinations for the number on the lid, using both colors.

  Example: #4 tub

  four red + zero blue

  three red + one blue

  two red + two blue

  one red + three blue

  zero red + four blue

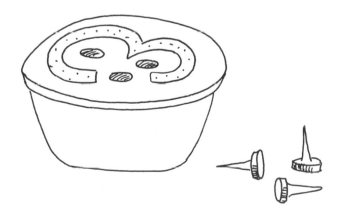

Two Feet Long

- Have each child trace around her foot on a piece of cardboard or tag-board.

- Show the children how to use their own foot to measure the length of the room, the art table, etc.

How Many?

- Provide a tub of water and several measuring utensils, such as measuring cups and measuring spoons. Also provide larger containers, like clear plastic liter soft drink bottles, and funnels.

- Let children experiment to see how many cups of water it will take to fill the larger container or how many tablespoons of water it takes to fill up a cup.

Inch by Inch

- Tape or paint lines on a classroom table one inch apart.

- Number the lines one-inch, two-inch, etc.

- Provide a variety of objects that are exact in inch measurements. (5" straw, 4" comb, 3" tube, 1" cube, etc.)

- Children match objects to lines to compare lengths.

Holiday Adaptation: Cut strips of construction paper in 1", 2", 3", 4", and 5" lengths. Children paste on art paper to simulate Christmas candles of varying length. Flames can be added with paint, crayon or construction paper.

Footlinks

- Paint and number lines at one foot intervals on the sidewalk or bike path.

- Children may measure objects or themselves.

- Children can also use them for jumping lines.

- The teacher can use the lines for stopping points for sharing riding toys.

    Example: "Jimmy, when you get to ten, it's Judy's turn to ride."

Bean Drop

- Use a felt tip marker to color one side of ten lima beans.

- Use the ten colored beans and ten uncolored beans,. Children spill the beans on the table and count the colored beans and the un-colored beans to see combinations that make a complete set.

- Let children begin with three colored beans and three uncolored beans; increase the number of beans as they increase in under-standing.

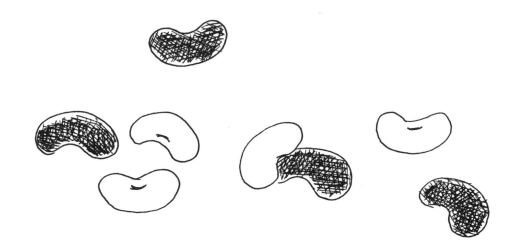

Living Sets

- Have children create sets by using their classmates as set members.

- For example, if the number five is being studied, have children cre-ate variations of that number by arranging classmates in sets of five — two girls, three boys or one boy and four girls, zero girls and five boys, etc.

218

Candy Counting

- Give each child a bag of multi-colored candies. Ask them to separate the candy into sets by color.

- Ask them how many green, orange, yellow, red, light brown and dark brown candies they have.

- Extend this activity further by asking children to count the candies into sets, for example, how many light brown and yellow ones they have, how many green and red ones, etc.

Crunchy Sets

- Give children a handful of different shaped crackers; ask them to separate the crackers into sets by shape.

- Ask children to count the number of crackers in each set.

Mud Cakes

- On a warm, sunny day, plan an outdoor activity in the sand box.

- Provide small buckets of water to make mud cakes and sticks (or real candles) to use as birthday candles.

- When children have each made a nice mud cake, ask them to place three candles on the cake.

- Ask them to add one more candle — ask, "Now how many do you have?"

- Continue the process at the appropriate level of understanding.

And One More...

- Allow the children to act out stories like *The Gingerbread Boy* and *The Big Turnip* which add characters to the story one at a time.

- After each new character is added, ask the children, "How many people or animals are in the story now?"

Egg Carton Shake

- Using a marking pet, place one to five dots in each of the sections of an egg carton. Put two beans, buttons, pennies, etc., in the bottom of the carton.

- Close the lid and shake the carton. Then open the lid and have the children count the dots together in the sections where the two beans have landed

Target Practice

- Cut the top off milk cartons on an angle at different heights, then staple the sides together to form a target with three or four sections. Numbers can be printed on the sections.

- Have children toss a yarn ball or bounce tennis balls into the target sections and add up the points.

221

Subtraction Action

- Sing songs and do finger plays with the children, such as "Five Little Speckled Frogs" or" Five Little Monkeys Teasing Mr. Alligator."

- Always let the children act out the songs as finger plays so they can visually see the results of one being eliminated.

In the Bag

- Number small paper bags (lunch bag size) from one to ten.

- Place objects in each bag to correspond with the numeral on the outside of the bag.

- Make several white cards or use small index cards and write -2, -3, -4, etc., on them.

- Lay one card down in front of each bag. Be sure the card has a numeral smaller than the one on the outside of the bag.

- Let the children draw a card and remove the number of objects from the bag and then count to see how many are still in the bag.

Do You Have a Brother or Sister?

- Prepare a simple graph that has a column for "yes" and a column for "no."

- Ask the children if they have a brother or sister, and mark the graph in the appropriate column according to the answer.

- Count the marks in each column, and ask the children if more classmates have a brother or sister or don't have a brother or sister.

What Did You Have?

- Prepare two types of juice — apple and orange.

- Ask children which type of juice they drank and allow them to mark the column on a graph that corresponds to their answer.

Color of the Day

- Cut six four inch squares of construction paper in red, orange, yellow, green, blue and purple. You will also need small wooden cubes in the six colors.

- Place the six colored squares on a table. As children come into the room ask them to take a cube of their favorite color and place it on the matching square of construction paper.

- If there is already a cube on their favorite color, then instruct them to put their cube on top of that one, as if to make a tall building.

- After all the children have participated in this activity, discuss with them which building is the tallest — which has the most cubes. The answer is the "color of the day."

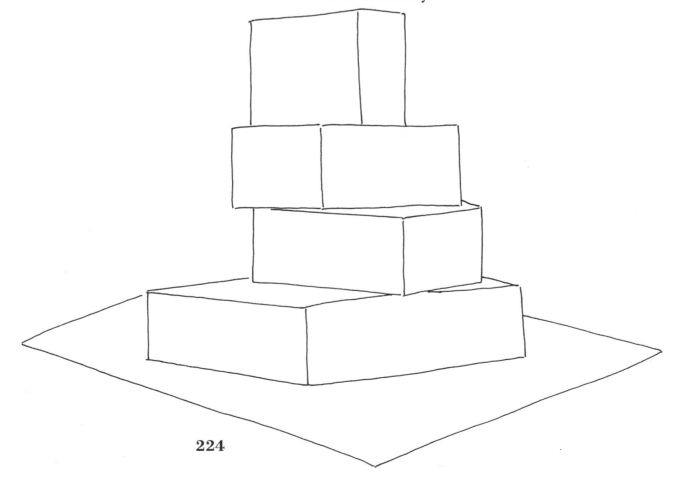

Popular Pets

- Poll children about their pets. (You may choose to have children who have more than one pet limit their contribution to one pet only.)

- Tally the results in a simple table. Be sure to include a "no pet" category.

  Example: Our Pets

horse	II	cat	IIIII II
fish	III	dog	IIIII IIII
mouse	II	guinea pig	I
turtle	I	no pet	IIII

Popular Pets II

- Give each child a plastic dog, cat, fish, etc. Children without pets can be given a small plastic basket to represent an empty pet bed.

- Write the names of the chosen pets on an already prepared graph form. Have children place their plastic animals or baskets on the graph.

- Use the graph for counting and comparing activities:

  How many children own cats? Dogs? Fish?

  Do more children own cats than dogs? Dogs than horses?

  How many fewer cat owners are there than dog owners?

  Are there more children who have pets, or more who do not have pets?

Symbolic Presentation of Data

- Many science and social studies projects offer the possibility of a pictorial or symbolic presentation of data. The following is one simple example developed from a study of peanuts.

- Prepare cards with a drawing showing peanuts containing from one to three kernels and a chart on which these can be displayed.

- Give each child a peanut to open, and have them count the number of kernels inside.

- Have the children find the card showing a peanut shell with as many kernels as their peanut has. The children then place the card in the column marked with a similar picture.

The Same
Amount
for Everyone

- Give the children a chocolate bar and ask them how the candy can be divided fairly.

- Children will mention the already existing lines.

- Break the chocolate bar on the lines and count the number of pieces.

- Tell children that fractions are used to divide things fairly.

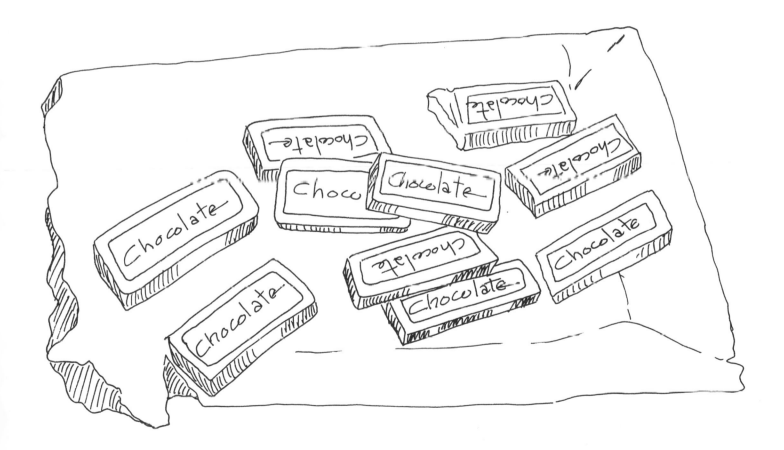

227

What Is a Half?

- Tell the children that one-half means dividing something fairly between two people.

- Illustrate this concept by cutting apples in half, cutting paper in half and pouring a full glass of water partially into a second glass so that each glass is half full.

- As each item is divided, ask the children one at a time which part they would want. The children should notice that it wouldn't matter.

- Cut the paper or apple into unequal portions and ask the same question.

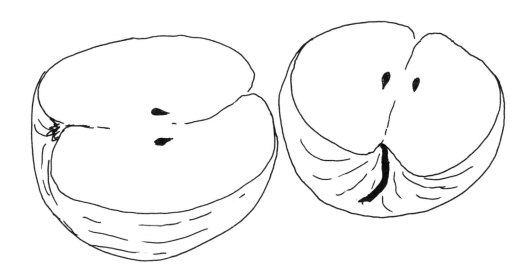

6

Music

ANYWHERE
AND EVERYWHERE

hildren develop confidence in their musical abilities by singing, playing rhythm instruments, moving to music, listening to music and being creative with music. Music provides a wonderful opportunity to reinforce other areas of the curriculum, such as reading readiness, dramatic play, math and large muscle development.

Singing — Children can sing with their teachers, with a record or all alone. It is important that singing efforts be appreciated. With exposure to opportunities to sing and with freedom to express themselves in music, children will develop confidence in their musical abilities. Songs for the preschool child should be accompanied with *activity*. Hammering with fists while singing "Johnny Works With One Hammer," fingercrawling while singing "Eency Weency Spider" or clapping, waving, swaying or stomping to any march tune are appropriate for this developmental stage. The preschool singer is *not a choir member*, but an active participant in musical activities.

Rhythm Instruments — Rhythm band instruments may be purchased or made. Instruments that make sounds can range from clapping hands, stomping feet, tapping fingers, to playing tambourines, beating drums and swishing pom-poms. Records and singing can provide accompaniment, but rhythm instruments can also be used alone, without accompaniment.

Movement — There are many opportunities to move to music. Marching, walking, bending, hopping, galloping, swaying arms are examples of large muscle activities that accompany music. Hand and finger activities to musical accompaniment provide opportunities for small muscles development. Moving like a rabbit, elephant or giant provides a dramatic play opportunity with music.

Listening — Listening to a song before trying to sing it provides an opportunity to hear melodic patterns and correct rhythms. Other listening may be done at the music center, in which children play records themselves, after proper instruction in the care of the record player. Music may be played at nap time and may also be used to denote transitions.

Creativity — Allow children to be creative in their response to music. They may initiate rhythmic movement or singing patterns that the teacher can reinforce. In this way, children will learn to enjoy music and develop their own musical capabilities.

Note: Songs and records for the pre-school child are readily available and very instructive. Therefore, a listing of songs and records is not included. This section will provide ideas that can be used and adapted by the "non-musical" teacher to teach the fundamentals of music — rhythm, dynamics, pitch, tempo and melodic patterns. These activities encourage creativity on the part of teacher and child and, hopefully, will encourage the child to transfer this creativity to other musical experiences. The activities encourage listening to music and learning to enjoy responding to it. The musical activities described also demonstrate the use of music to enhance other areas of the curriculum — fine motor development, large motor development, math, reading readiness, etc. Music can be a happy learning medium for the pre-school child.

Scarf Dancing

- Provide each child with a scarf (or long piece of lightweight cloth).

- Play a record.

- Children wave scarves to the rhythm of the music and move to the music.

- If scarves are not available, crepe paper streamers may also be used.

Magic Wand

- Provide each child with a scarf to use as a "magic wand."

- Begin playing a record.

- Direct children to wave their "magic wand" *over* their head, *under* the table, *between* their legs, *beside* a chair, etc.

* Reinforcement for positional vocabulary.

Preschool Limbo

- Play a record with a limbo or Caribbean melody.

- Children move rhythmically around the room in a line, going under a broomstick stretched across two chairs.

- Children should bend forward, instead of backward, for safety.

Grass Skirts

- Provide each child with a "grass" skirt made from newspaper.

- Make a "grass" skirt by cutting whole sheets of newspaper in strips, leaving a waistband at the top. Tape skirt together at each child's waist with masking tape.

- Allow children to respond freely to music.

Olympic Streamers

- Roll up newspaper into six inch wand; tape together to hold.

- Tape a long, thin strip of crepe paper to the wand.

- When a record is played, children make circles and other figures with streamers and move rhythmically around the room.

Giants and Elves

- Using a drum, beat loudly and softly, while children walk around room.

- Children tip-toe like elves to soft music, and walk like giants to loud music.

Preschool Fitness

- Put on a lively record and have children do a variety of large muscle exercises.

  Examples: While marching to music, "reach for the stars," "flap your wings" or march "like toy soldiers."

  While standing in a circle, bow, curtsy, or touch shoulders, extend arms.

Around the Chairs

- Place a line of chairs in the center of the room to make a traffic island.

- Put a record on and have children go around the chairs in different ways: walk, tip-toe, hop, skate, gallop, skip (if appropriate for group).

Butterfly Wings

- Tape four or five 10" to 15" streamers on a piece of computer paper.

- Make two long cuffs for each child's lower arm and tape, being sure that the streamers are flowing freely.

- When music is played, children can move around the room, fluttering their "wings."

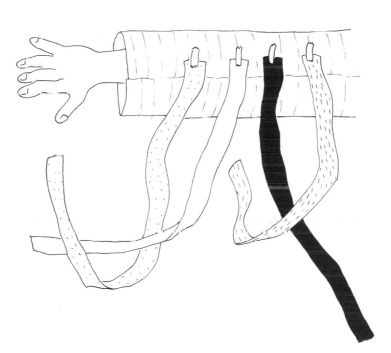

Musical Beanbags

- Give each child a beanbag.

- Put on a record. Children move around the room with the beanbag on their head, on their shoulder or on their elbow, while music is playing.

- When the music stops, the children "freeze" holding the position they are in until the teacher resumes playing the record.

Table Top Band

- Provide children with several objects to tap on a table in rhythmic response to a record — pencils, halves of stocking eggs, newspaper pom-poms, etc.

- For children to experience the variety of sounds made by instruments, teacher asks first for the pencil band, then the egg band, next the pom-pom band and even the fingertip band.

- For the finale (end of song) the children can choose their instrument; everyone plays together.

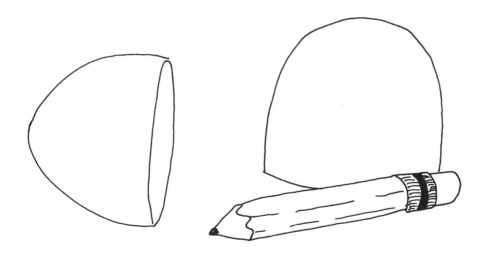

Leader of the Band

- Using a rhythm stick for a baton, let children take turns leading the class rhythm band.

- Roll up a newspaper to make a drum major's baton and let individual children lead the band, marching around the room to a record.

- Or use a smaller "baton" to lead a seated rhythm band.

Bottle Maracas

- Make a maraca by placing rice or gravel in an empty, clear plastic shampoo or detergent bottle.

- Glue the lid on for safety.

- Let children use the maracas as an instrument in the Rhythm Band.

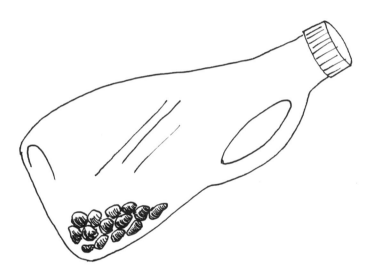

Drums and Sticks

- Use an empty gallon can with a plastic lid for a simple drum. Children can tap it with the eraser end of a pencil or with a stick that has a ball of cloth tied on the end.

- Dowel sticks may be cut into ten to twelve inch lengths to make rhythm sticks. Wooden kitchen spoons may also be used for rhythm sticks.

- Children play the sticks by tapping them on the floor or table or by tapping the sticks together.

Cool Music

- After making fans in a fine muscle or social studies activity, put on a record and let children fan to the rhythm of the music being played.

Circles to Music

- Provide each child with paper and crayons.

- Play a record.

- Ask the children to make circles to the rhythm of the music being played.

- Intermittently stop the record and ask the children to change to another color of crayon.

- The children will create a design of colorful circles, with a variety of interpretations.

Rhythmic Nursery Rhymes I

- Chant individual lines of nursery rhymes, putting equal emphasis on each word. Children repeat lines in same thythm.

- Claps could be added on specific words, such as those at the end of each line.

  Teacher: Ma-ry had a little **lamb.**
  Child: Ma-ry had a little **lamb.**

- Rhythm can be changed to one putting **emphasis** on every other syllable: Ma, had, lit, lamb.

Rhythmic Nursery Rhymes II

- Accompany chanted nursery rhymes with tambourine or tom-tom.

- Alternate chanted lines between boys, girls and entire group.

  Example:

  > *Group:* Jack and Jill went up the hill to fetch a pail of water.

  > *Boys:* Jack fell down and broke his crown.

  > *Girls:* And Jill came tumbling after.

242

Bongo Rhythms

- Create a rhythm by playing the bongo drum.

- Let children pick up the rhythm by "playing the table" with cupped hands.

- Other children can respond rhythmically by clapping hands, slapping thighs, stomping feet, clicking tongues or snapping fingers.

Pom-poms

- Prepare pom-poms by rolling half sheets of newspaper into stick shapes. Tape bottom half to form handle. Cut top half into strips.

- Play records with varying rhythms from marches to hulas.

- Children "swish" their pom-poms as they move to the rhythm of the music.

Holiday Adaptation: Have a Fourth of July parade using march music.

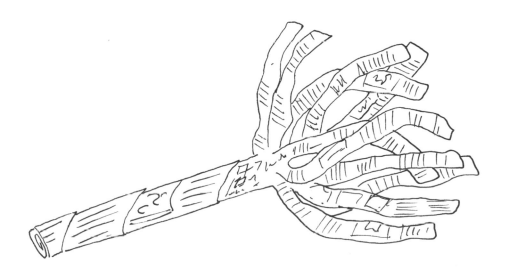

Pass the Pumpkin

- Seat children in a circle.

- Provide a plastic pumpkin for children to pass while the teacher beats a tom-tom.

- Children pass the pumpkin to the tempo of the music. Teacher alternates between slow and fast.

- When the music stops, the child who has the pumpkin stands and takes a bow. Process is continued.

Holiday Adaptation: This is a good party game. In addition to Halloween, it can be used for passing a wrapped Christmas present, a Valentine Box or an Easter Basket.

Freckles and Stripes

- Provide each child with a variety of crayons and paper.

- Play a record with a fast tempo and have children make dots on their paper in time with the music.

- Play a record with a slow tempo and have them make stripes with the sides of their crayon.

- Continue by playing both types of records, having children listen and decide whether it's freckle or stripe music before they use their crayons.

Friendship Circles

- Spread a long (ten to fifteen feet) sheet of butcher paper on the floor.

- Place children on both sides of the paper, each facing another child. Provide a variety of crayons for each child.

- Place a slow record on the record player. Tell children to make big, slow circles to the music with their crayons. Change the tempo by putting on a faster record. Children will color faster.

✱ Since two children will be using the same general space to color on the paper, they will have an interesting problem solving situation. They can synchronize their circular movement, or they can adapt their coloring movements to a smaller space.

245

Magic Crayons

- Have children get out their "magic crayons" (their fingers). Pretend they are putting rainbows in the sky.

- Using a record that has fast and slow passages, ask children to "draw" rainbows in the sky to the tempo of the music. Children make large arm sweeps back and forth as they "color."

Hi — Low

- Using a xylophone, let children respond descriptively with their bodies to the pitch of music.

- Arms up for high notes — Arms down to ankles for low notes.

- Stand up for high notes — Sit down for low notes.

- Walk on tiptoes to continuous playing of high notes — Bend over for continuous playing low notes.

Up and Down the Hill

- Play C D E F G A B C on a xylophone, or the song bells. Have children respond by raising their arms as the scale goes up; play the notes in reverse, and have children lower their arms as the scale descends.

- Continue with whole body movement, such as moving from touching toes to reaching for the sky and back again.

Happy Birthday

- When children have a birthday, include musical activities that relate to their years of age.

- Have a birthday choir. When Scott has his fifth birthday, he selects five people to stand and sing "Happy Birthday."

- Another musical birthday activity is the triangle salute. Jerri Lynn tells the class how old she is by tapping the correct number out on the triangle.

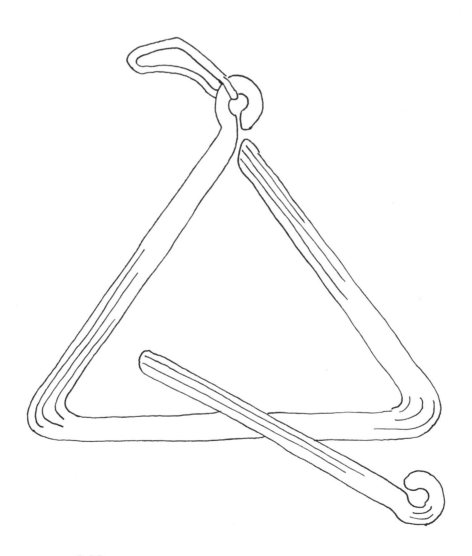

Variations on Old Time Favorites

- Adapt familiar songs to make them appropriate for teaching objectives or to individualize them for your classroom.

  Example: "Touch and Stretch"

  tune: "Mulberry Bush"

  objectives: large muscle development

  Verse 1: "This is the way I touch my toes, touch my toes, touch my toes. This is the way I touch my toes and that's the way it goes."

  Verse 2: "Stretch up *high* — touch the *sky*," etc.

A Healthy Song

- When children are learning about good food to eat, reinforce with this song. Sing to the tune of "She'll be Coming 'Round the Mountain:

  Verse 1: "We'll be coming to the table very soon.

    We'll be coming to the table very soon.

    We'll be coming to the table, we'll be coming to the table, we'll be coming to the table very soon."

  Verse 2: "We'll be eating _____ very soon.

    We'll be eating _____ very soon.

    We'll be eating _____, we'll be eating _____, we'll be eating _____ very soon."

- Children supply the name of a different healthy food every time verse two is sung.

Play Ball

- Place children in two rows about four feet apart.

- Let children roll a ball back and forth between the rows as they sing a song.

Different Voices

- To provide children an opportunity to hear their voices sound differently, have them put their hands over their ears while they sing.

∗ Variation: Have children put a hand, or both hands, up to their mouths while singing.

Sing and Listen

- Record children on the tape recorder while they sing.

- Re-play for children to hear.

- Teacher can add interest by having each child say his name into the recorder before the song.

Crescendo

- As children sing a song, use word clues (say "soft," "a little louder," etc.) to lead children through a song singing from very softly, to softly, to moderately loud, to loud.

- Using same clues, lead them back down from loud to soft.

- Teacher may reinforce word clues with facial expressions and ever widening or diminishing space between her hands.

Do As I Do

- Play singing games that allow individual interpretation and opportunities to lead, such as "Did You Ever See a Lassie?"

  Song: "Did you ever see a Lassie, a Lassie, a Lassie?

  Did you ever see a Lassie go this way and that?"

  Action: Children take turns demonstrating a movement, such a patting head, jumping, bending, etc. Group follows with same action.

Circle Songs

- While singing a favorite song, the children make a circle and move in circular fashion around the room.

✳ A variation would be two circles of children, one smaller circle inside a larger circle.

✳ A further variation would be several smaller circles of four to five children all singing and moving at the same time.

Divided Singing

- To vary a singing activity and to give children extended opportunities to learn new words, let various parts of the group sing the same verse.

  First time: All sing the verse.
  Second time: Children sitting in chairs sing.
  Third time: Children sitting on the floor sing.
   or
  First time: Boys sing.
  Second time: Girls sing.
  Third time: All sing.

Singing Stages

- Arrange physical settings that enhance the song and that encourage children to sing.

- Tape a rectangle on the floor and let children pretend it's a stage. Activity can be further enhanced by giving the children who want to sing a cardboard tube "microphone."

- To sing a train song, put chairs in a long row.

- While singing a boat song, children can sit in chairs placed in rows of two to "row the boat."

254

Windows

- Children make a circle and hold arms up to make "windows" while singing a song.

- One child at a time is chosen to go in and out the windows (under the arms) while the song is sung.

- When the verse is finished, the child goes to the middle of the circle.

Musical Clues

- For more effective and enjoyable classroom management, use songs played on the record player, sung by the teacher or played on a rhythm instrument to direct children to a specific activity.

    Clean up time: "Dance of the Sugar Plum Fairies" (Tchaikovsky) or "Time to Pick Up the Toys" (sung by the teacher) to the tune of "Mulberry Bush."

    > "Now it's time to pick up the toys, pick up the toys, pick up the toys.
    >
    > Now it's time to pick up the toys for all the girls and boys."

    Circle time: Taps on the triangle (teacher).

    Nap time: "Lullaby" (Brahms).

Happy and Sad

- Give each child two paper plate faces, one happy looking and one sad looking. Play records, or excerpts of records, that exemplify lighthearted, happy melodies and somber, sad songs.

- Children hold appropriate paper plate in front of their face.

    Holiday Adaptation: Use happy and sad pumpkin faces for Halloween.

Listening to Classics

- Select well-known classics, such as Tchaikovsky's Nutcracker Ballet, Beethoven's Fifth Symphony or Mozart's Minuets. Introduce songs at circle time and play regularly during quiet times, using correct titles and composers' names before playing.

- When the class is familiar with a few classics, ask which they would like played, again using correct names of composers and titles.

- * *Alternative:* At nap time, tune into a classical radio station for the children to hear.

Hummin' Birds

- Using a tape recorder, record the children humming a variety of familiar songs.

- Play songs back for the children to identify.

- Children can begin singing the words as they identify the familiar melody.

Classroom "Concerts"

- Send out a parent questionnaire that includes a question on talent.

- If some parents play instruments, ask them to demonstrate their instruments to the class.

- Another good resource would be fellow teachers.

- If performers are not available, perhaps parents or friends would show an instruments they have. Children could then touch it and hold it.

- Follow up with records that make individual instruments distinguishable. Ask: "Do you hear the trumpet?" "Do you hear the violin?"

Twin Tunes

- Have half of the class sing, "Twinkle, Twinkle Little Star," while the other side listens.

- Then let the other half of the class sing the "A B C Song."

- Alternate singing and listening.

- Have both sides sing at the same time, noting that the tunes are the same.

7

The Wonder of Wonder

CRITICAL THINKING AND PROBLEM SOLVING SKILLS

 hildren are born curious and capable of generating solutions to problems. Everyone has seen the young child, intent on reaching a toy, try various strategies until she gets what she wants. Every parent has experienced the endless maneuvers of a child trying to secure adult attention.

If this curiosity and creative problem solving are stifled by unintentional adult intervention, then the young child ceases to experiment with unorthodox approaches and looks to the adult for approved solutions. The critical steps involved with trial and error learning begin to be extinguished.

To re-stimulate the child's natural tendencies to generate multiple solutions to problems and to question the "why" and "how" of his world, the preschool teacher can create an environment conducive to this type of thinking. Activities in this chapter are designed to stimulate the child's natural ability to think critically and to encourage the teacher to follow processes that enhance this development. The alert teacher sets a tone for critical thinking by valuing alternate answers to questions, by refraining from offering ready solutions and by encouraging children to feel free to express their ideas.

The steps to problem solving are easy to employ with young children.

Step 1. Help children identify the problem. (The ball is in a mud puddle on the playground.)

Step 2. Encourage children to generate more than one solution. This portion of the process is a brainstorming activity, with no right or wrong answers. (A stick, another ball or a tricycle could be suggested for use in getting the ball out of the mud puddle.)

Step 3. Have children select one potential solution to test. (Group selects a stick for getting ball out of mud puddle.) It is important for children to verbalize their thinking. The teacher may have to say, "Why do you think that will work?"

Step 4. Allow children to test safe solutions. (They try knocking the ball out of the mud puddle with the stick.)

Step 5. Evaluate results of test with children by summarizing the results. Help them to determine whether the problem was solved effectively and efficiently, and to the satisfaction of the group. If not, repeat the process until a satisfactory result is obtained. (The stick moves the ball out of the mud puddle only if it's held at the end to make it long enough.)

The steps to problem solving can be used repeatedly throughout the day and without a formal activity to implement. Use teachable moments. *Situation* — Someone spills juice. *Problem* — What is the most efficient way to wipe up the spill? To encourage problem solving, the teacher must allow children to generate their own solutions.

Outdoor activities also provide many opportunities for social, as well as physical, problem solving. *Situation* — Bill and Bob both want a turn on the tricycle. *Problem* — How can both children have equal time on the tricycle?

In the area of critical thinking, the goal is to help children move beyond the naming and labeling stages of thinking and verbalization, and into application, analysis and evaluation. Children need to understand the why and how of their world. They need to be able to draw conclusions and predict outcomes based on their experiences and observations. With help from teachers who facilitate this type of thinking throughout their school years, children will be able to meet the challenges of successively more difficult problems. The preschool child who figures out five solutions for getting the ball out of the mud puddle may be the scientist of tomorrow who discovers alternative forms of energy, or the diplomat who successfully arbitrates peace between two warring factions.

Who's the Tallest?

- Have children look at their classmates and visually predict who is the tallest and who is the shortest member of the class?

- Record two or three predictions.

- Line children up. Have one child step out of the line and look at the others. Let that child find the shortest child by picking a child and comparing that child to the others. After the first child gets the line started, have another child take over.

- When the line is correctly arranged from smallest to tallest, let each child take a turn stepping out of the line and looking at the results.

Arm Stretchers

- Place a book on a high shelf or on top of a cabinet or locker out of the reach of children.

- Ask children to think of possible safe ways to reach the book.

- Pick a solution and try it.

- Evaluate the results.

- Follow the problem solving steps described in the overview of this chapter.

Will This Dissolve?

- Fill five clear glasses with water.

- Show children the following items: a rock, salt, a leaf, sugar and pepper.

- Ask children to predict whether or not the items will dissolve in water.

- Test each item with the children.

- Verify predictions.

- Adapt the problem solving steps described in the overview of this chapter to test each item.

Two Parts, Three People!

- Propose the following situation to the children: Mary and Jeff have just made a peanut butter sandwich. They used the last two pieces of bread. They cut the sandwich in half and were just getting ready for their first bite when into the room comes Randy. Randy would like some of the sandwich. What can Mary and Jeff do?

- Use the problem solving steps described in the overview of this chapter.

Tall Towers

- Give children five blocks of graduated sizes. Ask them to make a tower with the blocks.

- Talk about the variety of ways children build their towers, noting that there is more than one way to build a tower.

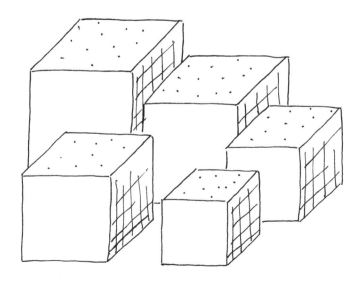

How Many in Your Family?

- After children have been introduced to one-to-one matching, give them each a baggie with several pebbles (six to eight) inside.

- Tell the children to take the bags home and match their family. Instruct the children to discard extra pebbles.

- When the children return to school, have them show how many pebbles are left in their bags.

- Make comparisons. Who has the most people in their family? Who has the least? How many children have the same number of family members?

What Can You Do With This?

- Teacher gives each child sitting in the circle a piece of paper.

- Teacher asks the children to think of something they could do with the paper, without moving from the circle.

- After giving the children time to think, teachers closes her eyes while the children do something with paper — tear it in half, crumple into a ball, put it under their foot, sit on it, fold it, etc.

- Repeat this activity at other times as children become more comfortable with trying original ideas.

What Will Go In This?

- Obtain three to four different size boxes; put something from the classroom in each box.

- As the teacher holds up each box, the children are asked to name things that could fit in the box. A small box might hold a matchbox car, a bracelet, a ribbon, etc. Repeat with each box and reveal the contents.

✳ Extend the activity by sending children home with a box to fill with something from home and bring back the next day. On following day, each child gets a turn having the class guess what's in his box.

Water Brigade

- Pose this question to children: "How many different ways could we take water from the water fountain to the water table?" Explain that children can use anything in the room to transfer the water.

- Let each child demonstrate a different method of her own creation (cup, spoon, baster, funnel with finger on spout, etc.). No one can repeat a process previously used, and the teacher does not suggest items.

- Encourage further thinking as children run out of ideas. "Is there anything under or around the sink that you could use?" (Paper towel (soaked and later squeezed), soap dish, wash cloth, etc.)

- "Is there any way that you could use your body to transfer water?" Cupped hands and mouth would be two possibilities.

Ping-Pong Volley Ball

- Place two long strips of masking tape on the floor — five feet apart.

- Ask children how a Ping-Pong ball could be moved from one taped line to the other without touching it. (Possibilities include blowing with your mouth, fanning with a book, blowing with a straw, blowing through a paper towel tube.)

- Let children try suggestions.

- Extend thinking to observing which method accomplishes the task the fastest.

- Use as a good rainy day game with one child on each side of line, moving the ball back and forth.

Stacks
and Stickers

- Cut a sheet of construction paper into a large triangle.

- Cut the triangle into four horizontal pieces.

- Give each child a set of the four pieces and eight to ten sticker circles (self-adhesive kind).

- Children use the sticker circles to put the triangle back together.

Holiday Adaptation: Use green construction paper and a variety of colored circles to make a decorated Christmas tree.

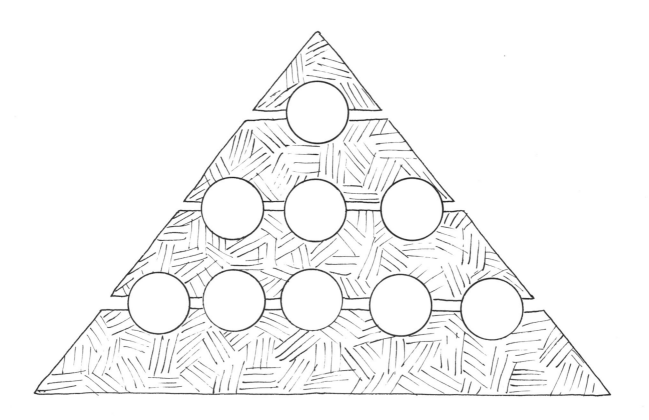

Candelabra

- Provide each child with a large white triangle cutout.

- Draw five candle holders.

- Provide five colored strips of paper (candle shapes) in seriated sizes: one tall, two medium height, two short.

- Ask the children to fit candles into "candle holders" so that candles don't go over sides of triangles. Paste.

Holiday Adaptation: Provide Christmas colors and make Christmas candelabra. Change the background shape and create a menorah for Hanukkah.

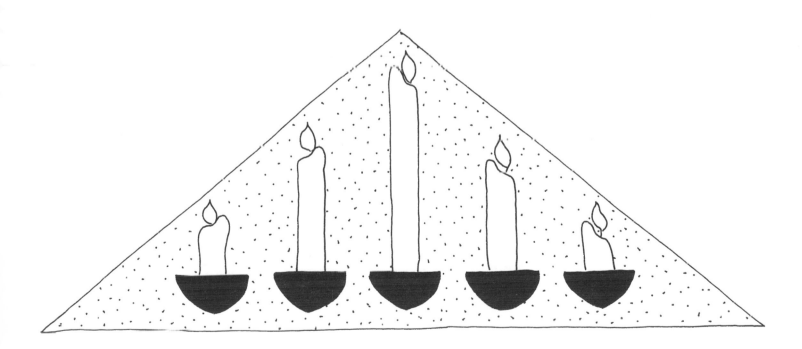

271

Where's the Birdie?

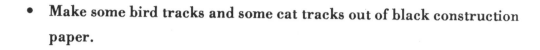

- Make some bird tracks and some cat tracks out of black construction paper.

- Tape the footprints on the floor with bird prints (about three pairs) going vertically and cat prints going horizontally, so that the two sets of prints meet at a right angle and then only the cat prints continue. Ask the children what happened.

- Children will guess many things, for example, the bird flew away, the cat ate the bird, the bird jumped on the cat's back, etc. Ask the children if there is any way they can know for sure what happened. Talk about clues.

Wacky Wednesday

- Read the story *Wacky Wednesday* by Theo LeSieg to the children on Tuesday. This book is a "What's Wrong Here?" type of story where everything is different from the way it should be.

- Tell the children that when they come to school tomorrow it's going to be "Wacky Wednesday." If they want to participate, they may do so by dressing in a way that is unusual, such as wearing a shirt inside out.

- On Wednesday, do several things to the classroom that are obviously unusual. For example, a table may be turned upside down or bulletin board characters could be reversed. Items could be moved from one center to another area of the room. The teacher could dress in an unusual way, such as wearing a pair of skates. Use your imagination, the wackier, the better.

- Let the children find all the things that are "wacky."

273

Is This Cup Full?

- Fill a glass with pebbles. Ask the children if the glass is full. If they don't think so, have them add pebbles until everyone agrees that the glass is full. Then ask if they think anything else will fit into the glass. The children will say no.

- Pour either salt or sand into the same glass. The children will be surprised to see the glass hold more. Call their attention to how the salt or sand fills in the spaces left between the pebbles. Now ask again if the glass is full. The children will say yes.

- Pour water into the same glass. The children will again be surprised. Ask if anybody knows why the glass could hold the water.

- Ask the children if the process could work in reverse, starting with a full glass of water and adding salt and rocks. Try their suggestions.

Separating Solids

- Mix one cup of beans, one cup of salt and one cup of rice together in a bowl.

- Provide the children with a strainer and a colander and tell them to separate the items in the bowl into three separate bowls — one with beans, one with salt and one with rice.

- After the children are successful, ask them if they can think of another way to accomplish the task.

Can Race

- Give children two coffee cans and several smaller items that can be placed inside the can, such as a block, a crayon, a roll of tape, a small book.

- Let children explore the way the item inside the can affects the can's ability to roll.

- Masking tape can be used to mark a finish line, and children can race their cans.

275

Spill Clean-up

- When a spill occurs, ask children how many ways they can think of to clean up the spill.

- Help children become aware of the steps they use to solve the problem. Problem — How can I clean up the spill? Possible solutions — Paper towels, mop or sponge (as many ways as children can think of).

- Select a method — Use a paper towel to clean up the spill. Test — Try using a paper towel. Evaluate — Did it work? Was it efficient?

- Think of other problems and have children go through the above process to solve them. (How to get a ball out of a puddle, how to share a triangle, etc.)

Sharing My Sandwich

- Ask children how they would solve the problem of dividing a sandwich between three people.

- Guide the children through the problem solving process of defining the problem, generating solutions, selecting one solution, trying the solution and evaluating the results.

From Many to One

- Give the children a set of nesting bowls.

- Ask the children how you could pack the bowls in a small box.

Puzzle Challenge

- Turn a puzzle over and have children put it together with the back-side up.

- Increase the difficulty by increasing the number of pieces in the puzzle.

Speedy Clean-up

- Deliberately spill a box of paper clips.

- Provide children with several items for cleaning up the spill, for example, broom, masking tape, dust pan, magnet, etc.

- Let the children experiment with each item to determine which item picks up the paper clips most efficiently.

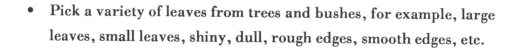

Leaf Sorting

- Pick a variety of leaves from trees and bushes, for example, large leaves, small leaves, shiny, dull, rough edges, smooth edges, etc.

- Put the leaves into one pile and ask the children to decide on a characteristic and put the leaves into two piles based on their selected characteristic. Example: large leaves and small leaves.

- Now ask the children to sort the two piles each into two more piles.

- Continue this process for as long as the children are able to think of ways to classify the leaves.

- This activity may be done outside. Circles could be drawn around each new group of leaves so that the children can see how the piles of leaves have developed. If the activity is done inside, the same pattern can be created on butcher paper.

- See if the children can reverse the process to get the leaves back into one pile.

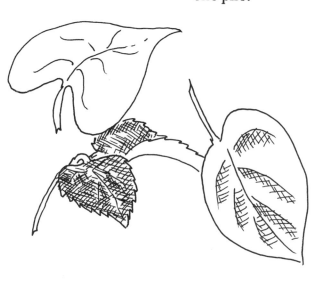

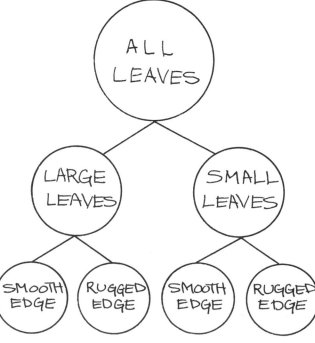

Funnel Race

- Roll sheets of paper into funnels with various sized openings at the bottom.

- Tape the funnels so that they retain their shapes.

- Let the children explore the speed at which the sand travels through the different sized funnels.

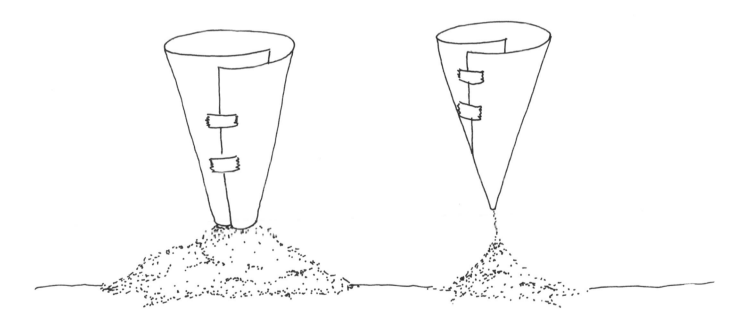

Squares and Rectangles

- Give children a line drawing of a rectangle three inches by two inches.

- Prepare six one inch colored square cutouts.

- Ask children to fit the squares into the rectangular space, pasting them so the entire rectangle is filled.

279

Triangles and Rectangles

- Cut out two four inch by two inch rectangles for each child — one white, one colored.

- Cut the colored rectangle into four triangles of equal size.

- Give each child a white rectangle and four triangles.

- Ask them to fit the triangles into the rectangle and paste.

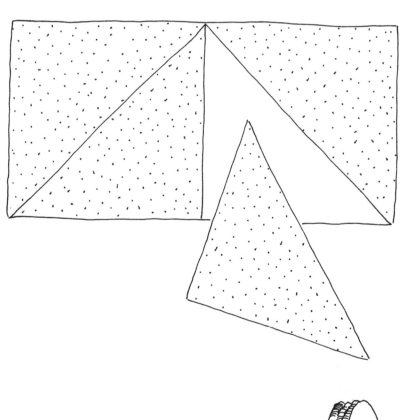

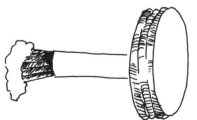

The Shape of Things

- Prepare a covered shoe box with a cutout on two sides — large enough for a child's hands to enter and manipulate objects.

- Place three to six wooden or plastic numerals in the box.

- Reaching in through the sides of the box, he feels the shape of numerals, and tries to arrange them in numerical order, left to right.

- Upon completion, he verifies his arrangement by lifting the lid of the box. If in error, he feels each shape by "running" his hands around numeral shapes, and tries the process again.

✳ This activity can also be done using larger numerals by putting numerals on a table and draping with a tablecloth.

The Eyes Have It

- Fill five glasses with water, four with tap water and one with cold water (no ice cubes, please).

- Ask children to identify the one glass holding cold water without touching them. Children should notice droplets on the outside of the cold glass of water. If unobserved, stimulate thinking by asking children to notice the outside of the glasses.

Holiday Adaptation: Wrap three to four items of varying sizes in holiday wrap. Examples: a crayon, a ball, a book, a doll. Display a duplicate set of items and encourage children to predict which item is in each box.

Greeting Card Cut-ups

- Cut up old greeting cards in puzzle-like shapes.

- Give each child a cut-up card and a background paper and let them fit the pieces back together to form a card.

Holiday Adaptation: Children's cards to take home at Christmas, Valentine's Day, Easter or birthday.

Picture Frames

- Cut pictures from greeting cards in a square or rectangle shape for each child.

- Provide three larger pieces of construction paper to each child in graduated sizes and in different colors. (Same shape as picture — square or rectangle.)

- Let child experiment with stacking the graduated paper sizes and the picture so that all colors and the picture will show.

- When child discovers relationship of paper sizes, she pastes them together.

Holiday Adaptations: Punch two holes in the top. String with yarn loop and use for Mother's Day, Father's Day or Christmas gifts.

What's for Snack?

- On days when snack has specific, identifiable aromas (cinnamon toast, bananas, etc.), bring snack in on tray covered by cloth.

- Let children take turns smelling and whispering their prediction in teacher's ear.

- Reveal the snack, verify predictions and eat. If the classroom is near the kitchen, while the food is cooking, let children predict the lunch menu. Verify predictions when lunch is served.

Pass the Purse

- Place three to five objects in each of several purses or paper bags (lipstick, emery board, bobby pin, marble, etc.).

- Pass the purses while a record is playing. When the music stops, each child holding a purse attempts to identify the objects without looking, by touch only. The child sitting next to purse or bag holder verifies the contents by looking. Continue music and passing.

Holiday Adaptations: Pass gift-wrapped boxes with holes cut in sides. Children identify gift or gifts inside.

Sound Casters

- On one day let children take turns making sounds with a variety of objects. Record on tape recorder. Crush paper, file nails, shake maraca, erase with pencil, etc.

- Save the objects used.

- On the next day, place the objects on a tray, play the tape and let children identify the object used to make each particular sound.

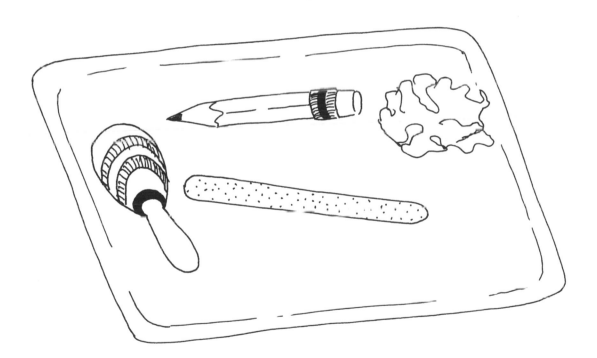

Taste Test

- Prepare popcorn for snack time.

- Divide popped corn into three bowls.

- Season one bowl of popcorn with Parmesan cheese, one with salt and one with sugar.

- Let children identify the substance on the popcorn in each bowl, after having had their three choices defined.

8

Moving Beyond the Horizon

DEVELOPING AN INTEREST IN SCIENCE

Developing an Interest in Science

Science for young children allows them to explore, manipulate materials, ask questions, discover cause and effect, project consequences and solve problems. It provides opportunities with both living and non-living things. Most importantly, however, the science area of the curriculum encourages children to learn about their biological and physical world.

An effective early childhood science program helps children to develop reasoning. The experiences cultivate children's natural sense of wonder and curiosity, and stimulate them further to find out more about the why and how of their world.

The classrooms and playgrounds are natural scientific laboratories when there are enthusiastic teachers to guide the learning. Teachers create a climate that allows children to ask questions and get answers, but, more importantly, they guide children in learning how to find out for themselves.

A developmentally appropriate curriculum allows children to have active involvement with plants, wind, friction, sound, changes of state, light, water, simple tools and machines, animals, rocks, gravity and other areas of the life and physical sciences. Children are encouraged to use their senses in discovery learning. In addition, the program provides opportunities for children to develop a sensitivity to the environment and the role they play in preserving it.

Scientific principles need not be learned in isolation. With knowledgeable teachers, these principles will be discovered as children participate in art, music, social studies, math, dramatic play and other areas of an integrated curriculum. Learning can take place both outside and inside the classroom, in a block center, during an activity, while eating lunch or resting on a mat. The alert teacher will also discover that scientific learning can be enhanced by taking advantage of the "teachable moments" that occur during the routine activities of the day.

The activities in this chapter provide first hand experiences for children to learn about science. The materials needed to implement the program can be obtained with a minimal expenditure of funds. Many materials may be obtained free, and most are already found in the classroom. With materials readily available, the enthusiastic teacher can provide a rich atmosphere for scientific thinking and learning.

Tom Sawyer Painting

- On water play day, give the children small plastic buckets of water and house painter's brushes.

- Let them "paint" the sidewalk, the side of the building and the wheeled toys. They will enjoy the "painting," but they will also discover that the water "goes away" — evaporates.

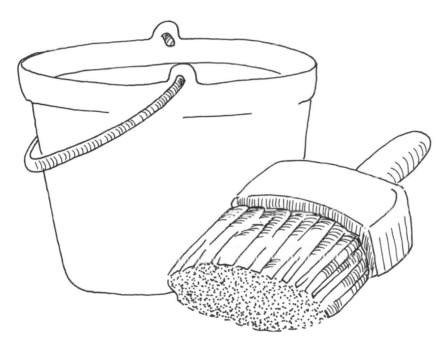

Old Fashioned Wash Day

- On a sunny day, prepare a big pan of soap suds and two pans of rinse water.

- Let children wash doll clothes or other small items on an old fashioned washboard. After rinsing twice, they hang the clothes on a line (or on the fence) to dry.

- Let the children take in the dry wash a few hours later; discuss the results.

Wind Wheels

- Cut a large circle out of a plastic lid so that only a rim remains.

- Tape strips of newspaper, crepe paper, ribbon or cloth onto one side of the rim.

- When outside, the children will be able to clutch the rim easily and run to make the streamers "fly."

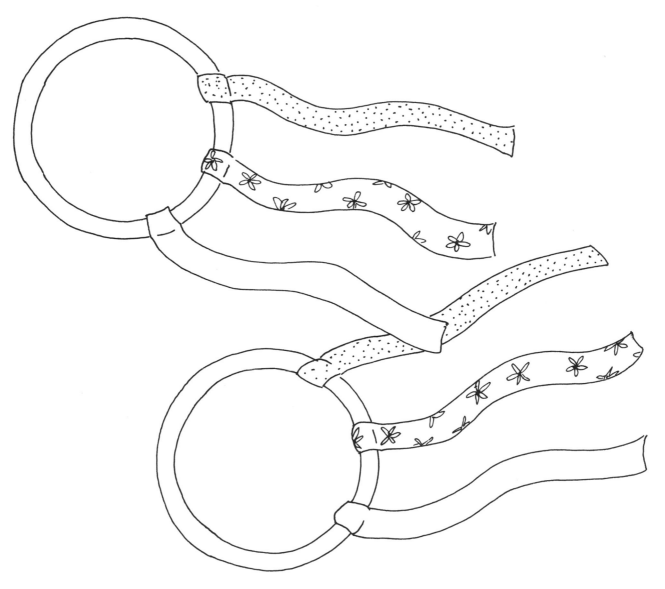

Wind Wands

- Roll up two sheets of newspaper to make a wand.

- Tape or glue crepe paper streamers to the wand from the mid-point to the top of the wand.

- As children run with the wand, the streamers flap in the breezes like a flag.

Holiday Adaptation: Using red, white and blue streamers, you have the "makings" for a July Fourth parade.

Air Conditioning Hoops

- Position a small fan in a spot that is safe for the children; place the following on a table: an embroidery hoop with cloth inserted, a shallow pan of water and a towel.

- After the children have dipped the cloth embroidery hoop into the water, they should place it on the towel to drip off excess water.

- Then they hold the hoops in front of the fan and feel the cool breeze on their faces.

Wind Walk

- Take a walk with the children to discover all the indicators that the wind is moving.

  Sample Questions:

  Is the flag waving?

  Is trash blowing around?

  Are people leaning into the wind as they walk?

  Do you see people's hair blowing?

  Are the trees and bushes bending?

  Is tall grass moving?

  Do you feel the wind on your face?

- Place a variety of objects on a table for children to discover how to move air and how to move objects with air: paper fans, straws, paper towel rolls, ping-pong balls in a long shallow box, empty plastic squirt bottles.

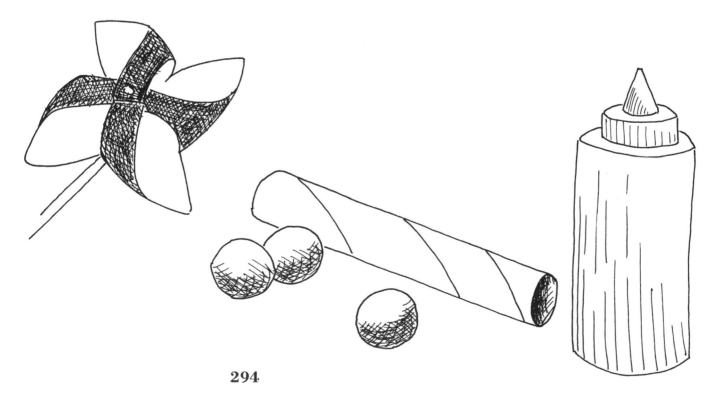

Sacks of Air

- Give the children lunch-size paper sacks to blow up.

- Have the children feel the sack and observe its fullness.

- After several blow-ups, let the children pop the sacks to let the air escape.

- Ask the children if they can think of another way to let the air escape.

Air Pushers

- Place small items, such as paper, feathers or styrofoam packaging chips in a circle of masking tape on the floor.

- Let the children take turns trying to "squirt" (push with air) the items out of the circle with empty plastic catsup, mustard or detergent dispensers.

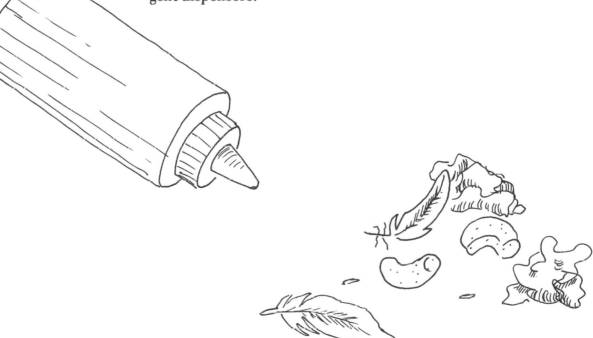

Raisin Elevators

- Pour clear carbonated soda water into a clear glass.

- Drop four or five raisins into the glass.

- After 40 to 60 seconds, children will observe raisins moving up and down in the glass.

- Teacher should help children draw the conclusion that the air bubbles caused the upward movement.

✱ Let children observe the glass later in the day when the carbonation has ceased. This will reinforce the role of the air bubbles in lifting the raisins.

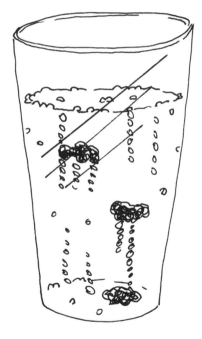

Bubble Machine

- Make a solution of soapy water, using liquid detergent in a small bowl.

- Give each child a straw and a turn to make bubbles in the bowl by blowing through the straw.

- Precede this activity with a lesson on blowing air through the straw as opposed to sucking air into it.

Down It Goes

- Give children several objects to drop — feathers, marbles, styrofoam packaging, small blocks, sponges, cotton, rocks, etc.

- After individual experimentation, help children draw conclusions based on their observations — which items dropped slowly and which items dropped quickly.

Cardboard Tube Slide

- Insert long cardboard tubes (from gift wrap, butcher paper or carpet rolls) into the sides of a large cardboard box.

- Place one at a level position. Place one tilted to the right side of the box and one tilted to the left side.

- Provide balls small enough to fit through the tubes.

- Let children discover that balls will roll down the inclined tubes, but not the level tube.

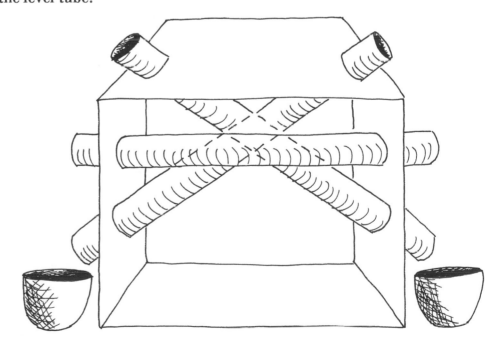

Downhill Racers

- Create an inclined plane in the block center by stacking two or three small square blocks and placing one end of a long (18" to 24") board on the blocks.

- Allow children to roll small balls, small cars or spools down the inclined plane.

- Provide additional blocks for further experimentation.

- Help children draw the conclusion that raising the height of the plane increases the speed of the rolling object.

Stringing Up

- Hang a string or piece of yarn from the ceiling.

- Provide one child with stringing beads or spools.

- Ask the child to string the beads and attempt to fill the string all the way to the ceiling.

- When beads fall, ask the child why. Explain that *gravity* is a force that pulls objects to the ground.

Invisible Names

- Children write names or draw pictures on butcher paper with cooking oil.

- When held up to a light source, names or pictures will become visible.

- Children can try to wipe it off with a damp sponge, but is does not go away.

Wave Maker

- **Demonstrate** this activity for the children. Use a clear plastic bottle at least ten inches high. Fill the bottle three-fourths full, using denatured alcohol.

- Add blue food coloring (enough to make it deep blue). Fill the bottle with cooking oil, leaving a small distance at the top. Glue the top on for safety.

- The substances will not mix and the water will move like a wave over the oil when moved up and down.

- Place the bottle on the table for the children's use, observation and questions.

Finger Paint Finale

- After children have finished finger painting, have a tub of water (or water table) ready to receive painted hands.

- Children will enjoy watching the color diffuse through the water.

- Color will change as more hands and different colors are placed in the water.

Color Bottles

- Using liter size plastic bottles filled with water, drop a few dots of red food coloring into the bottle. Cap well.

- Let the children roll the bottles back and forth across the table and watch the color diffuse through the water.

- Uncap the bottles and add drops of blue. Repeat the rolling process to observe the creation of the new color, purple.

- Place bottles in the window for room decoration.

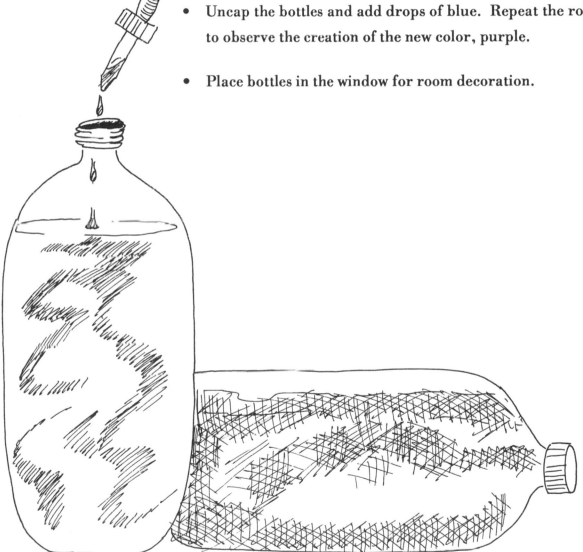

Soup and Soak

- Bring fresh vegetables to the classroom — peeled potatoes, fresh string beans, carrots, etc.

- After the children have washed their hands, pass the vegetables around so they can feel the texture and hardness. Let them snap the fresh beans.

- Discuss the names of the vegetables as the children place them into a cooking pot. Add water.

- Take to a kitchen to be cooked, or cook in the classroom in a crock-pot.

- When cooked, remove a sample of each vegetable. Let the vegetables cool so that the children can feel them again. Discuss the observations: "What happened to change the degree of hardness?"

- Serve for lunch.

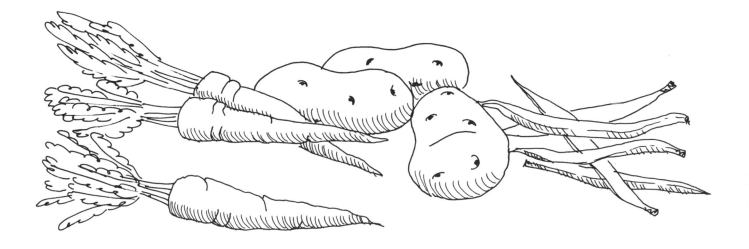

Ice in a Bag

- Let each child put an ice cube in a sealed baggie.

- Discuss how the ice feels hard and cold.

- Place the bags on a table until the cubes have melted. Talk about the change that has taken place, using the terms "solid" and "liquid."

- Place the bags in the school freezer (or let the children freeze them at home).

- On the following day, examine the bags again and discuss the changes that have taken place.

Soda Fizz

- Demonstrate the following activity: place a teaspoon of baking soda into an empty soda bottle (twelve ounce size) and add a teaspoon of vinegar. The two substances create a gas when they are mixed. This can be demonstrated by placing a balloon over the top of the soda bottle. It will expand from the gas. More of each substance will expand the balloon even more.

- Allow each child to mix the two substances. Provide a paper plate, a small cup of vinegar and a small cup of baking soda. Each child can use a spoon to put the baking soda on the plate and an eyedropper to add the vinegar. The mixture will fizz.

Holiday Adaptation: Use as "witches brew" for Halloween.

Jiggles

- Make gelatin with the class. Call attention to the solid state of the gelatin in the package. Have children note the change to a liquid when the gelatin is dissolved in water.

- On the following day, serve the gelatin as a snack, noting the change back to a solid.

- If less water is used than the recipe requires, the gelatin may be cut in cubes and be served as finger food.

Holiday Adaptations: Make red gelatin for Valentine's Day, green and red for Christmas and orange for Halloween.

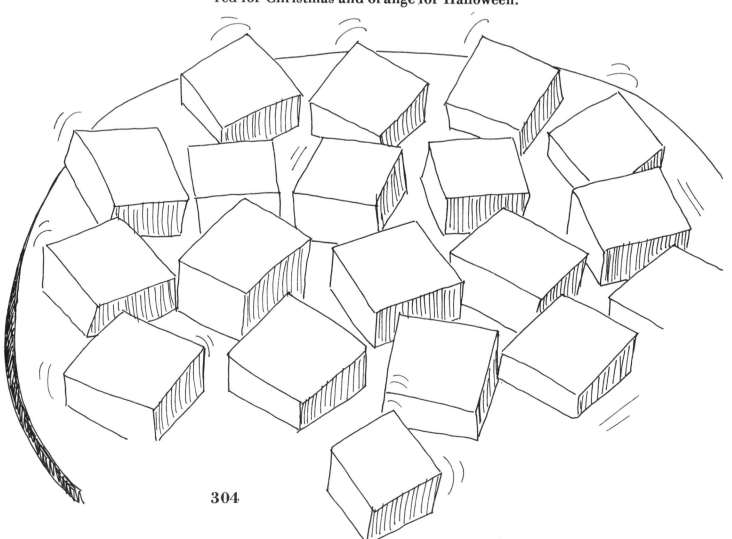

INTERESTING SCIENCE
LIGHT

Shadow Puppets

- Make a puppet stage by cutting a square out of the bottom of a cardboard box.

- Tape a white sheet of paper over the cut-out area.

- Turn the box on its side so that the square faces the audience.

- With a light source behind the box (projector light or strong flashlight), act out stories with stick puppets.

Guess Who?

- Using a sheet for a "stage front," have various people walk between a light source and the sheet.

- The audience sitting in front of the sheet tries to identify each mystery guest.

Holiday Adaptation: Use at Halloween for a costume parade.

Sun Art

- Children cut out a large design and place it on dark construction paper.

- Place the paper with the design in direct sunlight.

- After several days have children remove the design and note how the paper has faded.

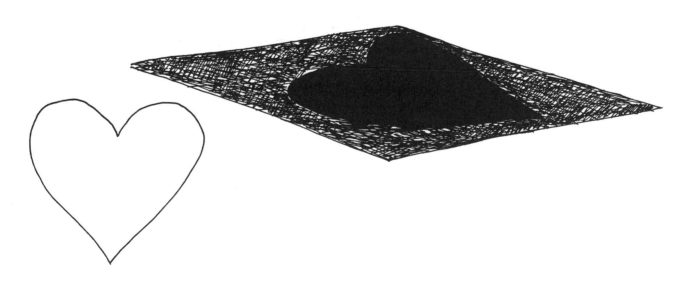

Rainbows Around the Room

- Hang a prism in an east or west window.

- When rainbows appear in the room, call attention to the source of the rainbows.

- Move the prism so the children see the direct relationship between sun, prism and rainbow.

Playdough

- Using your favorite playdough recipe, make two different batches of playdough — one colored red with food coloring and one colored yellow. (See pages 43 & 44 for recipes.)

- Give each child two playdough balls, one of each color. As children mix the two colors, they will discover the creation of orange.

- Continue with other colors.

Holiday Adaptation: Make pumpkins for Halloween.

Color Tubes

- Use a piece of clear plastic tubing, at least one half inch in diameter and 30 inches long.

- Put a cork in one end and fill with water. Add a few drops of food coloring and cork the other end.

- Remove the cork from the opposite end and add a different color. Replace cork.

- Wiggle the tube or turn it end over end; the color from each end will work to the center and mix.

Sanding Wood

- Give the children a block of wood with their name written on it and a piece of sandpaper. After the children have rubbed their sandpaper on the wood, question them: "How does it feel?" It should feel warm and smooth.

- Children will also discover that sandpapering erodes, or wears away, the surface when they see their name disappear.

 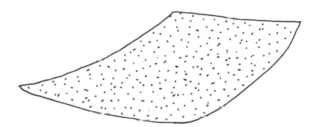

Shoe Skating

- Put on a waltz record and tell the children to "pretend-skate" across the floor.

- After the first record, have the children sit and discuss the experience: "Did some people find it easier to move across the floor than others?" Have the children look at the soles of their shoes; try to arrive at the conclusion that rubber soles are more difficult to slide across the floor than leather soles.

- Play another song, and let them skate with their shoes off. Compare socks and bare feet if appropriate.

- Have the children skate across a carpet and compare with a tile floor.

Megaphones

- Prepare a megaphone pattern as shown in the illustration. (This pattern must be enlarged.)

- Using heavy paper, let the children trace around the pattern and cut out if they are able.

- When megaphones are rolled and taped or stapled together, the children can go outside and practice "cheerleading."

✱ Make sure to caution the children against holding a megaphone close to another child's ear.

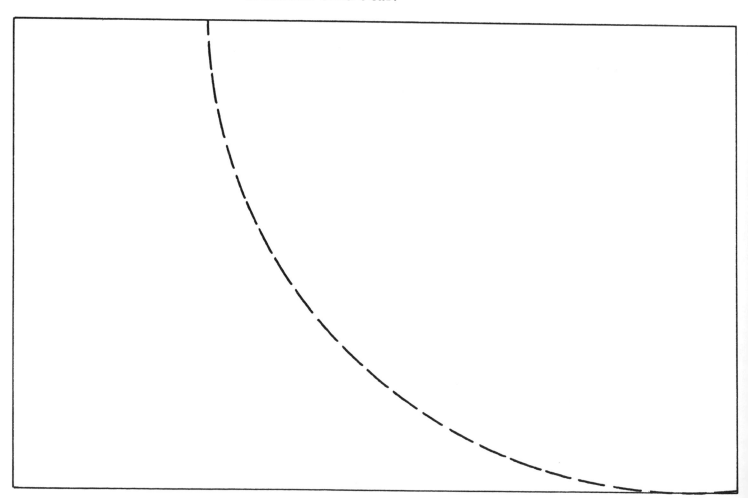

Listening for the Horses

- Ask children if they have ever seen a cowboy movie in which the Indian puts his ear to the ground to find out if horses are coming.

- Explain that sound carries through the ground and through other materials, such as table tops. The sound also sounds louder.

- Have two children sit at opposite ends of a long table and take turns scratching under the table. Have one child put her ear on the table while the other child scratches under the table. They will note how much louder the scratching sound is.

- A further use (and also a good group management technique) is to have children put their heads down on the table to listen for teacher's "scratching signal" to go to lunch, go to circle, etc.

Move That Water

- Using a water table or two plastic tubs, provide a variety of materials for the children to learn how to move water from one place to another.

    Examples: plastic bottles and jars

    plastic measuring spoons

    turkey basters

    plastic straws

    eyedroppers

    funnels

- If both short, wide plastic jars and tall, thin plastic bottles are provided, the children will gain experience in the cognitive skill of conservation of quantity.

Filter Game

- Using a water table or plastic tub, provide a variety of materials for children to discover how to filter or strain objects from water:

    Examples: styrofoam chips

    gravel of varying sizes

    leaves

    plastic colander

    tea strainer

    funnel

Kitchen Tools

- Bring items from the kitchen, such as a manual egg beater and a potato masher into the classroom.

- Set up opportunities for children to use these items to make work easy.

  Examples: egg beater and soapy water to make bubbles

  potato masher and banana to mash banana

Simple Machines

- To allow children to discover how to make work easier by the use of simple machines, set up the following in the block center:

- Suspend a rope and pulley in the block center so that the children can lift buckets of blocks in a basket. If your room does not permit this semi-permanent arrangement, make a temporary lift using two chairs, a broomstick and a plastic bucket on a rope.

Gone Fishing

- Tie a magnet on the string of a small fishing pole or rolled up newspaper.

- Place a paper clip on cut-out construction paper fish to attract the magnet.

- Place the fish in a small plastic wading pool or a "pretend" pond taped on the floor with masking tape. Let the children fish.

✳ To make an interesting variation, tape a boat shape on the floor, and let the children fish out of the boat (fish would be outside the boat on the floor).

Magnetic Maneuvers

- Make simple cardboard puppets, like paper dolls.

- Glue a paper clip on the back of the puppet.

- Create a background for the puppets, using a posterboard.

- By using a magnet behind the posterboard, children can move the puppets for the audience in front.

Toy Tows

- Attach a magnetic strip or disk magnet to the back of a toy car or truck and a washer to the front of a lightweight second car.

- Let children use the first car to tow the second.

Magnetic Hunt

- Ask children to look around their home and identify ways in which magnets are used in their home:

  Examples: magnets on the refrigerator to hold notes
  magnets on cabinet doors to keep them shut
  magnetic rims on paper clip holders to keep clips in

Rocks and Shells

- Prepare two small boxes for classifying rocks and shells by placing a rock in the bottom of one box and a shell in the bottom of the other.

- Place a quantity of rocks and shells on the table for the children to sort into appropriate boxes.

Making Sand

- Give each child two rocks to rub together.

- Place a sheet of dark paper on the table so that the children can see the sand that is produced by the rubbing action.

- By using a magnifying glass, children can see the rock shape of the sand.

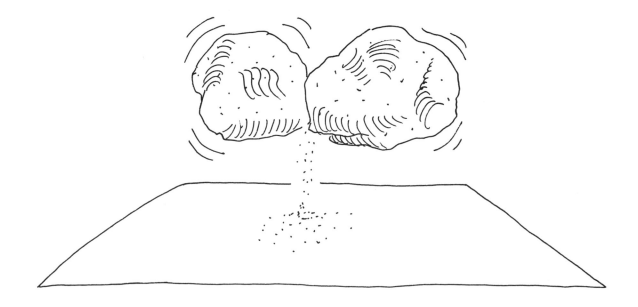

Tire Garden

- Make a tire garden on the playground by filling a tire(s) with garden soil.

- Let children plant flower seeds and take turns pulling weeds and watering.

- Enjoy the flowers when they bloom.

Vegetable Garden

- Plant carrots and onions in a tire garden on the playground, following directions on the seed packages. Have children water and weed the garden.

- When mature, pull up vegetables for children to see and feel.

- Cook, if appropriate, and eat.

Leaf Bracelets

- Wrap a piece of masking tape (sticky side out) around each child's wrist.

- Go on a nature walk and have children collect one leaf from each of several trees, sticking it on their leaf bracelet.

- When the class returns, sit in circle. Teacher holds up each leaf shape in turn and lets children identify similar leaf on their bracelets.

- Let children wear their bracelets home and check the types of leaves in their yards.

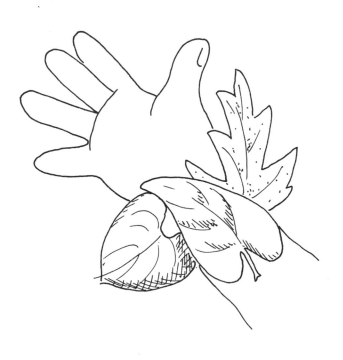

318

Grocery Sack Leaves

- Provide each child with a large square cut from a brown grocery sack.

- Display a fall leaf and discuss the variety of colors.

- Sprinkle several colors of dry tempera on the sack squares (red, yellow, brown, green, etc.).

- Let children mix the colors by painting with water and a brush.

- When dry, children trace around a leaf pattern placed on the painted paper and cut it out.

- The leaves can be used for fall bulletin board, or children can take them home.

Leaves — All Sizes, All Shapes

- Display baskets or boxes of different kinds of leaves: oak leaves, magnolia leaves, pine needles, willow leaves, etc.

- Encourage children to note differences in sizes and shapes of leaves.

- Let children take home a baggie with each kind of leaf.

- If appropriate, ask children to bring a leaf sample from their yard the next day. Pass those leaves around for comparison.

Leaf Rubbings

- To help children notice the veins in leaves and the different shapes of leaves, let them place a variety of leaves (underside up) under a piece of light colored construction paper.

- Using the sides of crayons that have had the paper covering removed, children make crayon rubbings of the leaves.

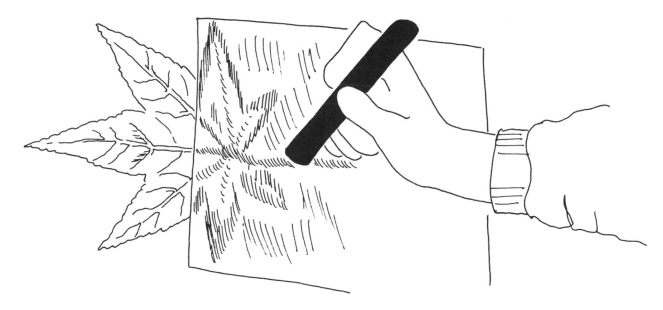

Treasure Hunt

- After giving each child a sack for collecting, go on a leaf treasure hunt in the playground or in the park. Assist children in noting that trees can be identified by their distinctive leaves.

- Place collected leaves in a large box on a table, and arrange shoe boxes on the table with a different leaf taped onto each box top lid (place lid upright at end of shoe box).

- Let children choose a leaf from the large box. Then they match it with a leaf on one of the shoe box lids and place the leaf in that shoe box.

Window Garden

- Let the children plant small plants in empty milk cartons, cups or clay pots.

- Discuss placement of the plants in sunny vs. shady areas.

- Keep eyedroppers and a bowl of water nearby so that the children can water (but not overwater) their own plant every day.

Egg Carton Planters

- Remove the top from a styrofoam egg carton; poke small holes in the cups of the bottom half so the soil will drain.

- Place the top of the egg carton under the bottom of the carton and use it for a saucer.

- Put potting soil in each cup and plant seeds. Water from the bottom, allowing the soil to soak up the moisture.

- Cover the top of the planter with plastic wrap until the seedlings appear. After germination, remove the plastic wrap and watch the plants grow.

- The children can measure the growth of their plants by marking the height on a popsicle stick stuck into the soil behind their plant.

Mini-Terrariums

- Cut a plastic liter size soft drink bottle in half. Remove the base from the bottom portion of the bottle.

- Let the children fill the base with gravel, aquarium charcoal and soil.

- Place a small plant in the soil and then water. Invert the remaining cut bottom half of the bottle over the plant to create the terrarium.

Little Sprouts

- Provide baby food jars, paper towels and lima bean seeds.

- Children place a dampened paper towel inside the baby food jar; nestle the lima bean between the folds of the paper towel.

- Place top on the jar.

- Children will be able to observe the bean sprouting.

- When sprouted, have children plant it in cup or garden.

Sweet Potato Vines

- To help children see the growth of roots and leaves, "plant" a sweet potato in a jar of water.

- Insert toothpicks in spoke fashion around the middle of the potato.

- Rest the toothpicks on top of a jar, with bottom half of the potato resting in water in the jar.

- Place in lighted area and watch the vine and roots grow.

What's a Nut?

- Start a display of nuts by bringing in a coconut and a pecan.

- Children and teacher can add to the display throughout the week, by bringing in walnuts, hazelnuts, etc. (Peanuts are not really nuts but are from the legume family.)

- Provide time for children to share and talk about what they bring.

- Extension can be developed by showing products produced from nuts, such as coconut oil and almond butter.

Natural Dyes

- One at a time, the teacher boils beets, broccoli, blackberries, coffee and tea, reserving the liquid to create dye.

- When cool enough to be safe for children to touch, the teacher shows the class which item produces which color.

- Children can dip strips of cloth into liquid to reinforce dye concepts.

Holiday Adaptation: Use dyes for dyeing Easter eggs.

Add a Tree

- To develop the concept that some trees change with the seasons, prepare a tree mural at the beginning of each season.

- Using butcher paper, draw a large tree shape and hang it on the wall.

- To emphasize seasonal changes, have children add appropriate collage bits or paint at the beginning of each season.

  Examples: Fall —brown, yellow, red, purple, orange paper bits

  Winter —bare tree with brown leaves on ground and gray painted sky

  Spring —popcorn buds and small green paper bits or paint

  Summer —fully covered with green paper bits or paint

- At the end of the year all four seasons will be represented on the wall display.

   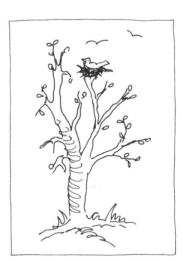

Spotlight on the Season

- Prepare a special place (table or shelf) to spotlight the seasons and seasonal changes.

- Arrange a basket of fall leaves and fall vegetables, evergreens with cotton snow for winter, a twig with buds (secured in a container of sand) for spring and a bouquet of greenery and flowers or a potted flowering plant for summer.

- As children bring in other items from home, add them to the display.

Feed the Birds

- To encourage childrens' interest in birds and to attract birds to the playground, let children take turns being responsible for throwing crumbs out for the birds.

- Seeds from fruit snacks can also be saved and placed on top of fence posts.

Bird Bath

- Obtain a shallow plastic pan or garbage can lid.

- Place in a safe, but observable, location in or near the playground.

- Pour water in container.

- Children can observe birds taking their bath.

- Caution children about observing quietly and not scaring the birds away.

Pine Cone Bird Feeders

- Spread wax paper on the table.

- Place a thin layer of smooth peanut butter on the wax paper.

- Children roll a pine cone in the peanut butter and then in bird seed.

- Attach a string to the pine cone and hang in a tree.

Holiday Adaptation: Hang a number of pine cones in a small tree with Christmas ribbon to prepare a Christmas tree for the birds.

Looking Loops

- Using cord or heavy string, make several loops by tying ends to make a circle.

- Place loops at various locations around the yard.

- Assign one or two children to each loop and ask them to look inside the circle and see how many insects they can see.

- Children can also be given a magnifying glass to assist in the observation process.

- Activity can be extended to look for rocks and plants, too.

Watch the Ants!

- After a picnic, leave chicken bones on the picnic table to attract ants. Watch from a distance.

- Children will be fascinated with the speed that ants arrive and start working to clean the bones.

- When ants are gone, teacher should remove bones to avoid harm to dogs.

Ant Helpers

- To remove odor from freshly collected seashells, the teacher can bury the shells in a can in the ground. Ants will clean off any remaining meat.

- Over a period of a few days, the shells will be cleaned, and the teacher will be able to dig up the can.

- Let children wash the shells and place on a table for display.

Bug Bottles

- To observe live insects, make a bug bottle from a clean bleach bottle.

- Cut out large circles in the sides so the insects can be observed.

- Place the cut-out bottle in a stocking and tie at the top.

- Release the insect at the end of the day so the children will learn respect for its freedom and life.

Habitats

- Prepare a large wall chart divided into three sections. In one section, have a picture of a meadow (or flat, grassy area), in the second section, have a picture of a tree, and in the third section, have a picture of water.

- Distribute pictures of animals to children and let them tell where the animal usually lives.

    Examples: cows, sheep, goats

    birds, squirrels

    fish, crabs, lobsters

Heartbeats

- Have children put their hands on their chest and feel their hearts (or use a cardboard tube to listen to a friend's).

- Put on a fast record and have the group do a lively movement exercise — then recheck the heartbeats in the same manner.

- Children should note that their hearts are beating faster, and they are breathing faster. Point out that exercise is good for a person's health.

- Have children check their heartbeats before they get up from nap. Point out the value of rest for their hearts.

Paper Plate Food Collage

- Have children cut out magazine pictures of food. (For younger children, the teacher may want to do the cutting ahead of time.)

- Place pictures in boxes that categorize food groups (vegetables, fruit, meat, etc.).

- Children then select something from each food group box to paste a balanced meal on their paper plate.

Tactile Temperatures

- Prepare a jar of ice water and a jar of warm water.

- Let children take turns touching the jars to see which is warm and which is cold.

- Children may close their eyes when touching the jars if they wish. This helps concentrate on using one sense.

Sound Canisters

- Fill film canisters, pill containers or potato chip cans with items such as rice, paper clips, beans or cotton to create sound canisters.

- Make two of each type of canister and color code bottoms for self-checking if desired.

- Children shake canisters and match those that sound alike.

Puffs of Smell

- Place cotton balls in several paper cups.

- Drop a different smelling liquid in each cup — vanilla, orange, peppermint and lemon extracts (or other substances safe to smell).

- Let children smell and identify.

✳ Activity can be extended by having children identify the lunch menu from the smells coming from the kitchen.

Taste Testers

- Have children close their eyes and perform taste tests on two cups of drink at snack.

    Examples: apple juice and orange juice
                water and lemonade

Follow the Arrow

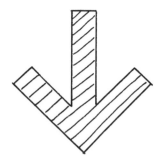

- Make a number of cardboard arrows — some straight, some right-angled and some left-angled.

- Hide a "treasure" or "treat" somewhere in the room or on the playground.

- Create a path with the arrows that will lead children to the hiding spot. (Be sure to place arrows far enough apart to challenge sense of sight.)

- Use and re-use.

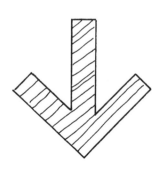

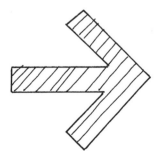

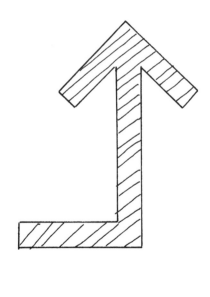

Sensory Alert

- Regularly play a game with the children in which you ask them to name things that they saw that were pretty or things that they touched that felt good or things that they smelled that were pleasing or things that they heard that were beautiful or things that they tasted that were good.

9

Everyone's a Piece of the Puzzle

AN APPROACH
TO SOCIAL STUDIES

An Approach to Social Studies

Social studies in the preschool begins with the individual child and the development of his self-esteem. When a child has a good self image, he recognizes his limits and his capabilities. He feels valued as an individual and will therefore function better in society at large. In addition, social studies develops an understanding of societal units and the roles of the unit members. This involves learning basic social science concepts and developing ways to establish and maintain relationships with other members of society.

Self-image — The teacher is the key to helping a child in the pre-school classroom develop a feeling of self-worth. The teacher's respect for each individual child furnishes the model for other children to follow. Each child is praised at appropriate times and encouraged generously. Correction is done in a calm but firm manner. Group interactions are guided in a responsible manner so that each child has opportunities to learn to lead as well as to follow.

Units — To help a child develop an understanding of the societal units in her life and the roles of the unit members, the teacher needs to provide materials, activities and situations that are related to *family*, *community* and *peer groups*. The home center provides opportunities for dramatic play related to family roles and rules. Activities, materials and stories that allow a child to have insight into the role of members of society, such as firefighters, police officers, post office workers, pharmacists, secretaries, store keepers, etc., contribute to these sociological concepts. Outdoor play time provides further opportunities to develop an understanding of family, community and peer group relationships. The alert teacher carefully guides play so that respect for rules and the rights of others is developed. Through incidental teaching, both inside and outside the classroom, the teacher has an opportunity to guide the development of effective peer group relations throughout the day.

Social Science Concepts — The basic understanding of economics, political science, sociology, history and ecology are being developed when a child plays store and trades articles; learns to be a leader and obey rules; develops an understanding of the role of each member of the family; becomes acquainted with different cultures; experiences holiday activities and other traditions; and learns to care for the environment. Opportunities to learn social science concepts can be provided through planned activities and incidental teaching throughout the day.

Relationships — The preschool classroom provides many opportunities for children to learn to establish and maintain positive relationships with other people. The classroom itself is a "mini-society," with opportunities to learn to work with peers, adults and systems. As children help with tasks, learn to follow school rules, respect the property of others, take care of property and materials, respect the rights of others, take care of their environment and learn social customs, they are learning to fit into a social order. Here, again, the teacher is the key. As a role model and organizer, the teacher can guide the small incidental situations and larger group situations into a good laboratory experience for the future adults of our society.

V.I.P. Treasure Chest

- Decorate a box to be a V.I.P. Treasure Chest.

- Make a number of happy faces on construction paper and cut out.

- At periodic intervals during the year, select a child to be the V.I.P. for the day, making sure each child has a turn.

- During a circle activity, allow classmates to take turns telling the V.I.P. what they like about him.

- Teacher acts as scribe, writing dictated phrases on back of each happy face. V.I.P. takes treasure chest home, filled with happy face phrases.

- Child returns the treasure chest the next day.

Follow the Leader

- Plan activities that allow each child to lead in the traditional "Follow the Leader" style.

  Example: When moving the class from one room to the other, let Doug choose the pattern of movement and lead the way.

      While waiting for lunch or snack, let Tiffany show the group things to do with their hands.

My Feelings

- Make a happy and sad face for every child in the room.

- Glue the faces back to back on a popsicle stick.

- Each morning, have children show the face that illustrates how they feel.

- Randomly choose a few children to tell the group why they feel the way they do.

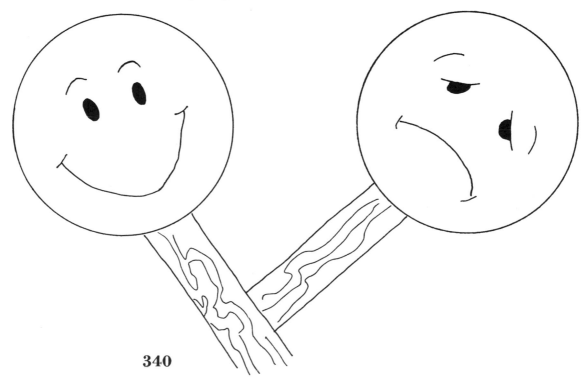

Name Tree

- Let children trace around each other's hands on green paper.

- Cut out the hands.

- Write each child's name on her hands.

- Arrange on the wall in the shape of a tree, by starting with the bottom row and then overlapping successive rows like house shingles.

Holiday Adaptation: Place a star on top and paint tips of fingers red to make a decorated Christmas tree.

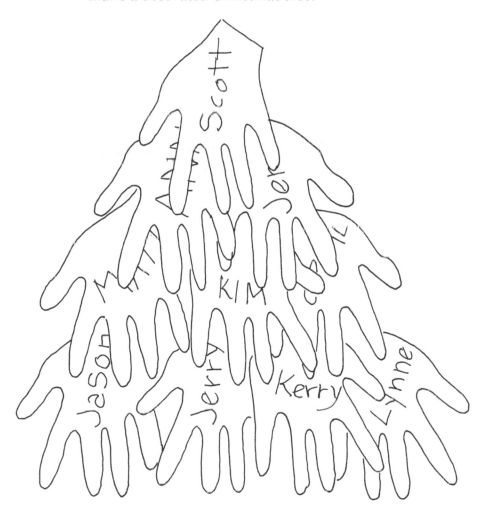

Family Portrait

- Allow each child to draw all the members of his family.

- Label each family member as they are described by the child.

* This activity can be extended by allowing each child to tell about his family to the group.

Holiday Adaptation: If you are having a Thanksgiving event at school, this makes a great display.

Paper Doll Family Crowns

- Pre-cut paper dolls and allow each child to pick one doll for each member of her family.

- Cut strips of grocery sacks sufficient in length to go around children's heads to make a headband.

- Let each child glue the family members (paper dolls) to the headband, making a family crown.

Growing Up

- Have each child bring a picture of himself as a baby, a toddler and at present age (magazine pictures can be used if necessary).

- Discuss what a child can and cannot do at each age.

- Sequence pictures chronologically on a chart.

Family Tree

- Ask children to bring pictures of grandparents, parents and themselves.

- Place family groupings in chronological order as children talk about their lineage.

- If inappropriate for group, use magazine pictures to categorize age groups.

343

Responsibility Roster

- Develop a Responsibility Roster by preparing a posterboard with several rows of glue-on picture hanger hooks. Over each hook is written a chore, for example, wipe tables, bring toys in, straighten book shelf, etc. (A small picture by each chore is helpful to amplify directions.)

- Write each child's name on a three by five inch card. Punch two holes in the card and insert yarn to create hanger.

- Children choose a chore for the week by hanging their card on the chore of their choice.

Responsibility Straws

- Label a series of juice cans with a list of chores — for example, wipe tables, straighten books, pick up trash in yard, sweep sand off sidewalk, etc.

- Place cans in a box which is labeled *Chore Box*.

- Place straws that have each child's name written on a flag in the box.

- When children come in on Monday, they choose their chore for the week by placing their "flag straw" in the chore of choice.

- Provide time for chores to be accomplished and acknowledged.

Trash Truck

- To help develop experience in sharing responsibilities for group living, prepare a trash truck by punching holes in a box and inserting a small rope tied as a handle.

- Paint sign on side of box — *Trash Truck.*

- Children take turns pulling Trash Truck around yard (or classroom after snack) for classmates to place trash in "truck." Driver empties trash in can.

Litter Brigade

- Use a cereal box and cord to make litter collectors for each child to hang over his shoulder.

- Go for a walk as a group, with each child carrying a litter collector to fill with items that have been thrown on the ground. School grounds remain clean due to efforts of the Litter Brigade.

Traffic Lights

- Prepare green, yellow and red circles.

- Discuss what each means — green/go; yellow/watch out; and red/stop.

- Children paste the circles in a shoe box lid in the order simulating real traffic signals.

Stop Signs

- Give each child a piece of construction paper with a stop sign shape drawn on it (eight sides).

- Write the word, STOP, in black wax crayon inside the drawing.

- Let children sponge over or paint the sign.

- Children cut out the sign.

- Use the sign as a prop with tricycle traffic.

∗ Reinforcement: Ask children to count STOP signs on the way home.

Use and Re-Use

- To help children understand that items can be re-used, send each child home with a grocery sack and a note asking parents to help children collect items that can be re-used, for example, plastic butter tubs, clean bottles, egg cartons, corks, soap bits, old stockings, etc.

- When items are returned to class, sort into categories that are related to use.

- Use items for many activities described in other chapters as well as for the activities in this chapter.

Re-Cycled Products

- Involve parents in saving these items for school use.

Item	Use
Window Envelopes	Use for individual collections of leaves, alphabet letters or pictures.
Meat Trays	Use for art activities, like crayon drawing trays.
Computer Paper	Use for art paper.
File Folders	Use for individual art folders.

Sack Suits

- Cut holes in paper grocery sacks for child's head and arms.

- Let child paint or color on front of sack.

- Put on a record and let children have a sack suit parade to show off their creations.

Holiday Adaptation: Stuff sacks with newspaper. Tie together with green yarn. Paint sacks orange to make giant pumpkins. Have a pumpkin patch for Halloween.

Can Collection

- Send a note home asking parents to help children save aluminum cans.

- Start a collection of cans in a large box.

- Ask for children and parent volunteers to take cans to re-cycling center each week; receipts are brought in by "child volunteers."

- At the end of the project, show pictures of items that can be bought for the room with the proceeds. Group selects an item, and the teacher buys it for the classroom.

Sandbox Tools

- Use clean bleach bottles to make buckets, sand scoops and funnels.

- To make buckets, cut the bottle in half and use the bottom of the bleach bottle.

- To make a scoop, use the top half, with handle. Screw on cap.

- To make a funnel, remove cap from the top half of bottle.

Re-Bow

- Use old gift wrapping bows to make flower leis when doing activities related to Hawaii.

- Cut a cord (or ribbon) necklace length; string bows on cord.

Corkers

- Re-use corks collected by children for:

  floating in the water table

  counting and gluing on paper plates in sets

  gluing on collages

  stoppers in bottles

Get a Ticket

- As children prepare to come in from play, tell them they need a ticket (a piece of trash) to enter the door.

- Teacher stands at the door with a trash can, collecting tickets and commenting, "Wow, you picked up a lot of tickets!" or "Doesn't our yard look nice now?"

Hand Washers

- Encourage children to bring soap bits to school, instead of throwing away.

- Collect soap bits and place in a stocking.

- Tie stocking with soap bits to handle of sink for use as handwashing soap (also keeps soap off the floor).

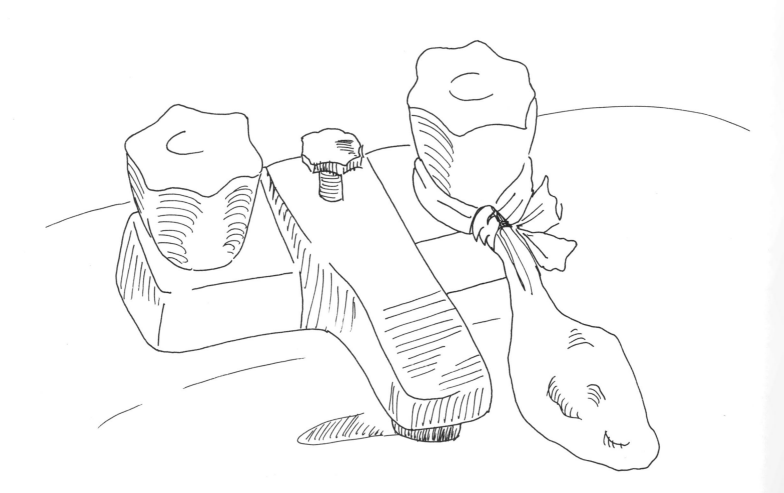

Bits and Pieces

- To help children learn how to save materials, keep a container on the art shelf for bits of paper that are leftover from cutting activities.

- Establish a practice with the children of tearing these scraps into little bits and saving them in the container for future collage activities. (A clear plastic container makes the project more interesting for the children because they can watch the "bit" pile grow.)

Rainwater Resource

- To help children learn to use available resources:

- Place containers on the playground to collect rainwater.

- Let children use this collected water to water plants in the room or on the playground.

- Inch markings may be placed inside the container to show how much rainwater has been collected.

Mini-Forests

- Obtain a number of small trees (five to ten inches in height) from friends, parents or your personal yard. Acorns that have sprouted, tallow trees that have "volunteers" under them or small pine seedlings are examples of usable types.

- Bring the small trees to the classroom and let children plant them in cut milk cartons.

- Children water the trees and keep in sun.

- After a period of growth, the trees will need to be re-planted. Let each child take a tree home to plant. If yards are not available to children, plant on school grounds or in the yards of "friends of the school."

- Discuss with children that years from now other children will enjoy the trees, animals will make homes in them, etc.

Letter Carrier

- Make "mail boxes" for backs of each child's chair by folding a large piece of construction paper into a pouch and taping it together. Write child's name on mail box.

- Have envelopes prepared with a child's name printed on each.

- "Letter Carriers" may place previously cut magazine pictures in envelopes or teacher's messages to parents before delivering to backs of chairs.

Holiday Adaptations: Deliver Valentines and Christmas cards this way.

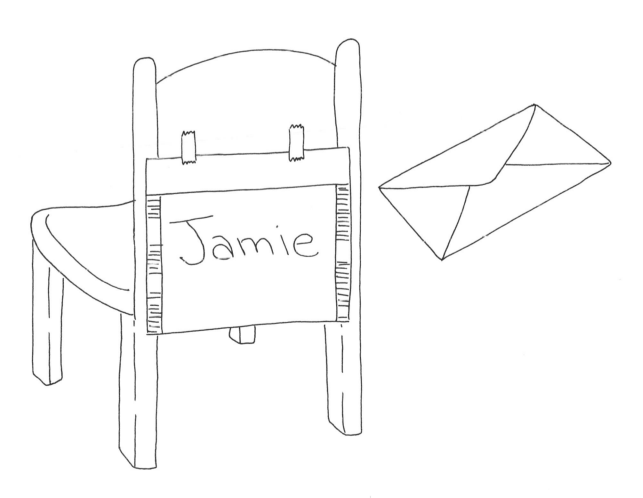

Job Fair

- Invite parents (or individuals) from the community to visit the class and tell what they do on their job.

- Encourage speakers to bring something tangible for each child to take home, or touch and see, that is related to their work, for example, pharmacists — a pill bottle, banker — blank check, pilot — picture of plane, computer programmer — computer paper, etc.

- This will encourage children to verbalize information about careers at home.

Prop Boxes

- Develop a variety of prop boxes for various careers and professions. Each box would contain dramatic play equipment for that specific job. There could be a box for medical careers, a box for secretaries, a box for teachers, a box for bus drivers, etc. Each box could be brought into the dramatic play center for a week or two at a time so that children could develop their own play.

  Example: Beauticians and Barber's Prop Box: play phone (for receptionist), calendar book (for receptionist), pencil (for receptionist), plastic hair rollers, hair dryer (with cord cut off), razor (without blade), capes, cardboard scissors, electric shaver (with cord cut off), mirror.

School Bus Driver

- To create a bus, use a large refrigerator box. Cut out door and windows and paint tires on box.

- Leave in the room for a week while children take turns being driver.

- Use the opportunity to teach safety rules for getting on and off bus.

Sidewalk Art Sale

- Save children's art work for a period of time and mat it.

- Clothespin art work to a fence or place on the hall walls with price tags of five to twenty-five cents.

- Invite parents and friends to the sale.

- Place proceeds in a class "kitty."

- After the event, take children on a field trip to convert art sale money into ice cream treats.

Small Mall

- Have teachers bring garage sale items for children to sell out of refrigerator box store (or table) — keys, old necklaces, scarves, baseball caps, etc.

- Let shopkeeper place previously prepared price tags, ranging from one to ten cents, on items so children can count out money.

- Children get pennies from "banker" and pay for items, which they take home.

- Shopkeeper returns pennies to "banker" at end of day to be re-used on next day. Continue for a week or until items run out.

- After sales, allow children to trade if they wish, so they can learn concept of bartering.

Pass it Along

- With parents' cooperation, have a hall or sidewalk "garage sale" to pass on outgrown clothes and small household items. Price at two, five, ten, twenty-five cents and a dollar so children can develop experience with money recognition and selling as they work as shop-keepers.

- An alternate method would be to sell books and magazines.

- Let children select a new classroom toy from a catalog with the proceeds.

From Here to There

- To begin a discussion on transportation, ask children if any of them have moved. "How did your furniture get to your new house?" "If you wanted to send a toy to a friend who lived across the ocean, how would you get it there?"

- Ask similar questions to elicit answers, such as moving van, truck, trailer, ship, airplane, etc.

- Let children cut pictures from magazines and glue on a *Transportation* mural.

Let's Vote

- Display three phonograph record covers.

- Give each child a small removable stick-on note.

- Children vote for the record they want to listen to at naptime by placing their tab on the record cover of choice.

- Count votes. The record with the greatest number of tabs wins.

Holiday Adaptation: Prepare a chart showing three ways a pumpkin can be carved into a jack-o-lantern. Children vote by placing a gummed label with their name on it in the column under selected pumpkin face. Pumpkin is carved in the manner selected by most votes.

Mock Vote

- During a presidential election year, allow children to simulate the voting process in the classroom.

- Talk about each candidate and the party they represent.

- Describe symbols (elephant/donkey) related to each party. Cut out elephant and donkey shapes from paper.

- Give three *very broad* platform areas for each party.

- Allow children to wear elephant and donkey shapes home each day.

- Have pictures of each candidate in the room. At the end of the week allow children to vote.

- Make a ballot from divided posterboard with the picture and party symbol for each candidate. Place the ballot in a private place and allow children to go one at a time and place an X under the photo of the candidate they support. Announce the results.

✷ This activity teaches vocabulary and concepts, i.e., election, political party, vote, ballot, etc., that are a beginning for better understanding of the voting process.

Senior Citizens Day

- Invite residents from a local retirement center to visit the classroom and maybe have lunch.

- Allow time for children to sit and talk to individual seniors.

- Ask each senior to share with the class what they did when they were preschool age.

✷ Activity can be enhanced further with the sharing of childhood pictures by the seniors.

By-Gones

- Have children ask family or neighbors to help them locate an item that was used in the past, but has been replaced or is no longer needed in modern society.

- Have children bring items to class to share with classmates.

    Examples: flat iron

    butter churn

    hand fan

    manual juice squeezer

    coffee grinder

    wash board

    lantern

    button hook

Home Visits

- Take a field trip to various homes — an apartment, a two-story home, a one-story home, a mobile home, etc.

- Discuss what was unique about each one.

- Begin a picture display and let children cut out pictures of different kinds of houses.

- Conclude with children that families live in many types of homes.

This is Home, Too

- Begin a picture display of homes that children may not have been in, for example, an igloo, a thatched-roof cottage, a houseboat, a house on stilts, a lighthouse, a wigwam, a jungle hut, etc.

- Reinforce with stories and poems about families living in such homes.

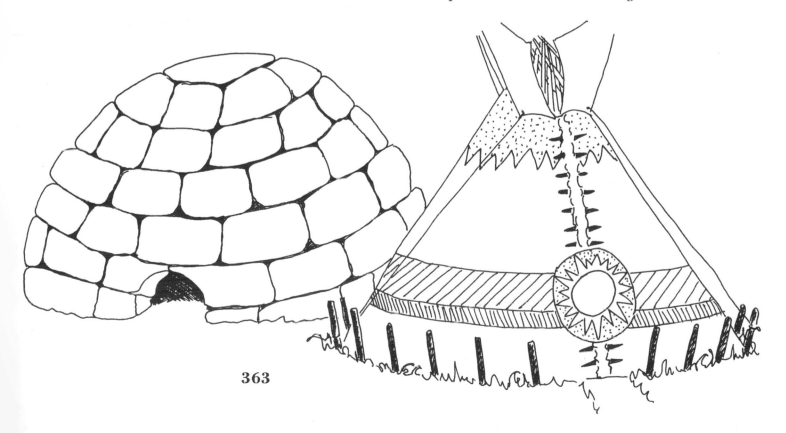

An Accordion Display

- To create interest in and understanding of people of differing cultures, prepare a series of pictures of people involved in interesting, but different, activities, for example, someone washing clothes in a river, eating with chopsticks, dressing in a sari, carrying a baby on a cradleboard, etc.

- Glue the pictures on manila folders in a vertical position. Cut tab side of folder to make it even.

- Hinge the folders together with tape. When all the folders are opened, one long line of pictures will be displayed in accordion fashion.

- To create additional interest, place the "string" of folders on the floor in a semi-circle. Children can lie on the floor and look at the pictures.

- Teacher could be nearby to answer questions and stimulate discussion.

See, Touch and Hear

- At various times during the year create interest centers based on a particular culture.

- In addition to displaying pictures, have a bonsai plant, fans, teapot and teacups, tatami mats, chopsticks, geta slippers, etc.

- Plan an activity involving the children, such as painting on construction paper and folding into a fan.

- Also, on that day read a children's book about the country.

Honored Guests

- To help children develop a respect for cultural diversity, invite parents or friends of the school from various ethnic backgrounds to visit the school and talk about their customs, show pictures, perhaps, teach a song or game.

- If visitors bring items of clothing, the visit will be even more interesting to the children.

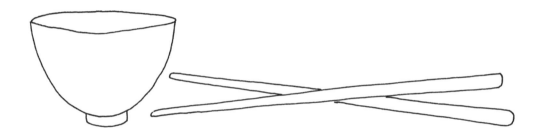

Adios and Sayonara

- Since children are learning language very rapidly at the early childhood stage, begin a year-long process of learning yes, no, good-bye, one, two, three, four, five or other appropriate words in a foreign language.

- Ask parents, friends or children in the classroom for help in teaching the teacher.

- Many teachable moments arise throughout the day, when a response to a question or a request can be given in another language. "May I have another cookie?" "Si."

366

International Costume Day

- Celebrate a special International Day to extend an awareness of various cultures.

- Children can wear ethnic costumes, such as Mexican sombreros and serapes, African Togas, Japanese kimonos, Native American "deerskin" skirts/pants/moccasins, Indian saris, etc.

- Classroom parents or friends can serve as consultants.

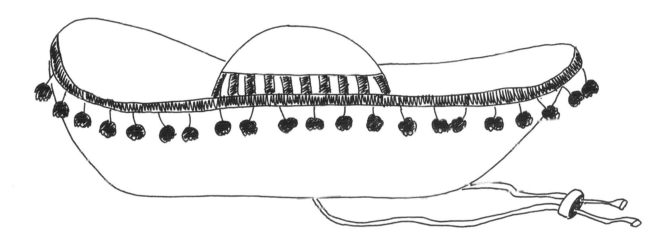

International Feast

- Plan an International Feast Day that would have a variety of foods for children to sample, for example, Japanese tea, Polynesian poi, Mexican enchiladas, African yams, Chinese egg rolls, Italian pasta, Jewish bagels, cream cheese and lox, Polish sausage, etc.

- Arrangements could be made with school staff, or parents could be involved if appropriate.

- A parent-involvement covered dish supper could be planned as an option.

367

Fiestas and Other Special Celebrations

- With the help of friends or parents, teachers can commemorate the significant celebrations of cultures represented in the classroom or community.

- Food, games, music or special activities could be planned to celebrate such special days as Mexican Cinco de Mayo, Jewish Purim, Korean Cherry Blossom Festival or the Chinese New Year.

Happy Birthday, America

- On July Fourth prepare a cake and put candles on to equal the age of the USA. Children sing "Happy Birthday" to the United States to give meaning to the holiday.

- Prepare a line drawing of a US flag — one big enough to tack to the wall as a mural. Let children glue old red and white gift wrapping bows on alternate stripes. Paste a blue background on star portion of flag. Children glue on white bows for stars. Explain that the stars represent the states.

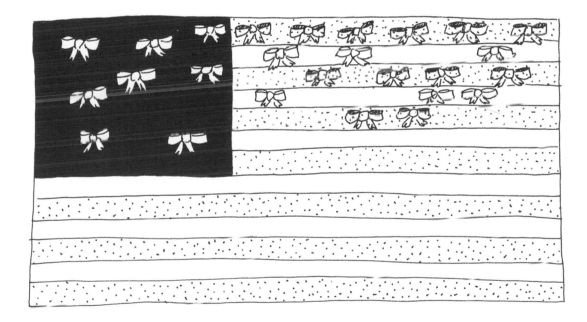

Hints For Teachers

- Many opportunities are available for the insightful teacher to help children develop a feeling of self-worth.

- **I'm glad you're here:**

  To help children know they are valued as an individual, begin each day and continue throughout the day with activities that focus on the individual child:

  Greet each child by name at the door.

  Bend down to talk on her eye level.

  Listen to her comments and respond accordingly.

- **Special Box:**

  When children give you their drawings and other "treasures," help them know they are valued by keeping a Special Box for such contributions.

  The box should be visible and attractive.

- **You're an important member of the group:**

  Place child's name on cubby hole or coat hook.

  Display each child's paintings, not just "best" ones.

  Be sure that each child has an equal turn to be a leader and a helper.

- **Accentuate the Positive:**

  Find opportunities to praise each child in an honest and positive manner.

  Avoid using comments that label a child or compare one child's abilities to another's.

  Examples: "Richele, I'm so proud of you."

  "You really tried hard, David."

  "I like the way you're putting the blocks back neatly, Latasha."

  "Katie, would you do it this way next time?"

....

(Also see holiday activities listed in the index.)

SEPTEMBER

OCTOBER

DECEMBER

JANUARY

FEBRUARY

MARCH

APRIL

MAY

JUNE, JULY, AUGUST

Index

Story S-t-r-e-t-c-h-e-r-s:
Activities to Expand Children's Favorite Books

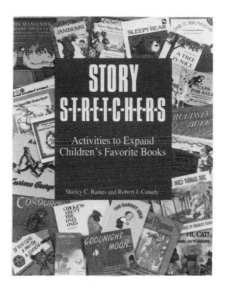

Shirley C. Raines and Robert J. Canady

Children love to hear and look at good books. Here is a perfect way to connect children's enthusiasm for books with other areas of the curriculum. *Story S-t-r-e-t-c-h-e-r-s* are teaching plans based on the stories in outstanding picture books that are among children's favorites.

Here are 450 teaching ideas to expand the interest of 90 different books. These ideas are organized around eighteen units commonly taught in the early childhood classroom.

"*Story S-t-r-e-t-c-h-e-r-s* is the best thing to happen to story time in decades. It should be the bible of every preschool and early primary teacher in America. Even better, it can be used just as easily by parents. Nothing I've seen approaches it in practicality and originality."—Jim Trelease, Author of *The New Read Aloud Handbook*

ISBN 0-87659-119-5

Do Touch: Instant, Easy, Hands-On
Learning Experiences for Young Children

LaBritta Gilbert

This unique book of hands-on activities is designed to surround children with things to explore, wonder about, do and discover. These activities can be prepared quickly and easily from simple materials such as cups, sponges, craft sticks, corks, rice, and sandpaper. The chapters focus on pairing and puzzling, forming, fitting, categorizing, measuring, sorting and more. Clear directions and objectives are aided by expert illustrations.

ISBN 0-87659-118-7

More Mudpies to Magnets:
Science for Young Children

Elizabeth A. Sherwood, Robert A. Williams, Robert E. Rockwell

Here are 200 more pages of ready-to-use science experiments. The science skills developed by the activities in this book include classification, measuring, using space and time relationships, communication, predicting and inferring, and numbers. The chapters include:

- Chapter 1—Colors, Crystals, and Creations: Chemistry Beginnings
- Chapter 2—How Things Work: First Physics
- Chapter 3—Digging in the Dirt: Earth Explorations
- Chapter 4—How Hot, How Cold, How Windy, How Wet: Weather Watchers
- Chapter 5—Aerial Acrobatics: Flight and Space
- Chapter 6—Roots and Shoots: All About Plants
- Chapter 7—Houses for Snugs, Hideouts for Hamsters: Animals Adventures
- Chapter 8—Hodge Podge

ISBN 0-87659-150-0

The Learning Circle:
A Preschool Teacher's Guide to Circle Time

Patty Claycomb

Hundreds of circle time activities make this a necessary book. Activities can be used again and again because they give children a chance to talk about themselves and their friends. There are learning circle activities for every month, day, and season. Patty Claycomb knows how to weave a spirit of magic and adventure into the daily classroom.

ISBN 0-87659-115-2